PRAISE FOR GONE TO

M000159328

"The stories in this book offer moving memories and reflections on the lives of mothers, seen not only from a child's perspective but from the eyes of an adult who has been living without their mother since childhood. These narratives give a captivating insight into the many layers of the mothers; as a parent, a child themselves and a young adult and the new connections that the authors often find through the process of writing about them. It reminds us of the power of a loss and how even after many years, memories and stories are an important aspect of remembering and grieving."

-Suzannah Phillips, Associate Director, Winston's Wish
www.winstonswish.org

"These poignant stories of mothers gone too soon infuse childhood loss with a poetic transcendence, each sensitively layering a portrait of a young woman through the eyes of her child. Of particular note are the author reflections that follow each story, bringing adult perspectives and wisdom to the indelible experience of early mother loss. For the bereaved of all ages who have wanted to write their own story, this book provides an accessible structure."

-Kathleen Adams LPC, PJTR, Registered Poetry and Journal Therapist
President, The Center for Journal Therapy, Inc.
Author, *Journal to the Self and Journal Therapy for Overcoming Burnout*

"With this beautifully written and informative anthology, the authors of My *Mother's Story: Gone Too Soon* are offering mental health professionals, educators, families and the public at large—an international audience—the opportunity to learn and understand the impact of parental loss on children from adults who were bereaved as children. By sharing their stories and insights, the authors shine a light on common myths about children's grief and mourning and also strategies that foster resilience. They have also informed us of how it impacted their lives into adulthood and continues to impact their lives today.

As the CEO of Alex Cares Inc., I steward our belief in the power of young people to explore and understand their story in the face of loss. This exploration creates a meaningful canvas for youth to find the tools and resources, that help them realize that their loss is not their whole story, but a key piece to what and who they will become.

My Mother's Story: Gone Too Soon is an inspiring and thoughtful anthology filled with compassion and wisdom. While the collection focuses on the loss of a mother in childhood, I firmly believe that the insights offered by the authors are applicable to the experience of loss and grief for anyone at any age and offers a healing tool for all of us."

-Amy Liebman Rapp, M.S.Ed.,CT
Childhood Bereavement and Youth Development Authority

CEO Alex Cares Inc./Alex Cares for Grieving Youth® - The Sanctuary National Grief Support Network

Founding Board Member, National Alliance for Children's Grief (NACG)

Founding Board Member and former Managing Director. A Little Hope – The National Foundation for Grieving Children, Teens, and Families

"These authors have beautifully captured the essence of their mothers. What an honour to read these 'love poems' to the moms of left-behind adult children - they are precious pieces of writing. Even more poignantly, it is clear in the author reflections that they have moved through a searching and grappling process to face the trauma of losing a mother so young, and through what otherwise could have remained frozen grief. Already a strong believer in the power of narrative and journal therapy, I will be recommending *My Mother's Story: Gone Too Soon* to the bereaved that I work with. These are unique resources that will inevitably encourage meaning-making and healing through grief."

- Devony Baugh, Registered Clinical Counsellor, Vancouver, Canada

My Mother's Story:

GONE TOO SOON

Published by Mothership Stories Society March 2022
New Westminster, BC Canada
ISBN: 978-0-9879844-3-2

Editors:	Michelle Hohn & Marilyn Norry
Typeset / Layout:	Red Tuque Books
Cover Design:	Hallographix Design & Multimedia
Printer:	Island Blue Book Printing

Other Books by Marilyn Norry

My Mother's Story: The Originals (2012) Contributing Author & Editor
My Mother's Story: North Vancouver (2012) Editor
Writing Women's History: Starting with Your Mother (2018)

Published Stories by Michelle Hohn

"The Story of Florence"; Original Version (2015)
"Abundance"—*Chaos to Calm: Awakenings Through Covid-19* (2020)

Mothership Stories Society
mymothersstory.org

"Mother is the first world we know, the source of our lives and our stories. Embodying the mystery of origin, she connects us to the great web of kin and generation…

…when we hear these stories, we tap into the wisdom of our Motherline."

-Dr. Naomi Ruth Lowinsky
*The Motherline: Every Woman's Journey
to Find Her Female Roots*

This book is dedicated to our mothers,
and all who seek to connect—or reconnect—with
the comfort and wisdom of their Motherline.

CONTENT WARNING

In addition to the consistent anthology theme of early mother loss, this book contains a range of life experiences and specific topics that some readers may find difficult, including: substance use/abuse and death by overdose, domestic violence, mental illness, sudden or unexpected death, terminal illness, fatal accidents, self-harm, death by suicide, and wartime brutality.

My Mother's Story:

GONE TOO SOON

Edited By Michelle Hohn & Marilyn Norry

CONTENTS

FOREWORD

Gone Too Soon is the third anthology of *My Mother's Story*, a project I started in 2004 to tell women's history, starting with the story of our mothers. All the stories in this project follow a simple writing recipe based on storytelling found in dramatic writing.

That's my world. As an actor, I play other people—imagining what it's like to be a character with a background, ambition, context, or even gender different from my own. As a dramaturg/story editor, I work with playwrights and screenwriters to help them craft stories with thrills and spills, laughter and tears, and clear motivations. In my world the chaos of life is filled with facts or elements waiting to be framed into stories.

In 2004, few of the stories being told in the scripts I read or the films I saw were about women making decisions in their lives or finding the courage to deal with their circumstances. I couldn't relate to the simplicity of most of the female characters and written history didn't provide many alternatives.

Then I was at a wedding and a friend told me the story of her mother's life—not her opinion or issues, just the facts of where and when her mother was born and what happened next. I heard this as a character arc, a device we use to track the physical and emotional journey of each character in a script. Wondering if we might find some interesting women's history, I asked my friends, female actors in Vancouver, to write the facts of their mother's lives from beginning to end. I imagined most of these stories would be somewhat like my mother's since we, the daughters, now found ourselves in similar circumstances but, really, I had no idea what we would discover.

The results were surprising on so many levels—unique stories of women living throughout the 20th century, from around the world, all classes, races, religions, rich, poor, troubled, living through wars both outside and inside the home, through abuse, adoptions, addictions. These were the stories of rich complexity I was looking for and they were everywhere!

We read them to one another and agreed this was the best theatre ever. So, we staged many readings of these stories and had workshops asking for more stories from the community. This led to an online archive managed by our non-profit society, and through that, we published two anthologies: *The Originals* and *North Vancouver*.

One of the other surprising aspects of this project was the benefit gained by the writers. The 'assignment' compelled writers to talk to friends and family to research their past. Putting facts in order meant taking themselves out of a story they had only seen from their own perspective. They came to see their mothers as human beings like themselves, and this became a step of individuation. Many could see patterns in their families, like seeing the forest rather than the trees, and this opened new levels of discussion with different generations of family.

You might think this project would be a sure-fire success, but the truth is that most people don't want to talk about their mothers. They say, "What a lovely idea… for someone else." I'm fascinated by this reticence; as far as I can tell, it's true in cultures around the world. It speaks to a huge taboo people feel against disclosing details of their mothers' lives, as if saying anything will bring great shame to them, their family, and to their mothers. I felt it too when it came time to write my mother's story. It takes courage to break through this taboo, and most people need strong motivation to attempt it.

When Michelle approached me with the idea of *Gone Too Soon*, I knew it would succeed, if only through her passion. From the start, she recognized the value of the writing recipe and the stories that emerged—although her background gives her more insight into the journey of the writers than my focus on the story of the mothers.

I was so impressed by how, after writing her story, she started training like an athlete with course after course, including counselling credentials, so she would feel ready to guide people through grief and bereavement, and whatever else might come up. You have no idea what will come up when you ask people to tell the facts of their families. The beauty of using the writing template is that it's about storytelling—how can I best tell the story of the events of my mother's life—rather than processing. Michelle made sure she was equipped to deal with it all. And she's done just that in many contexts, including hospice workshops and private practice. We regularly meet to discuss the myriad aspects of the past, present and future of *My Mother's Story*.

For this book, though, I had some reservations. It fit the tradition of this project that we embark on a path that hadn't been done before. We already had a few stories written by people who were bereaved in childhood (and two of them are in this book). My father lost his mother when he was five and wrote his mother's story at age 85, so I was somewhat familiar with the experience.

However, this would be our first book bound together by the mothers having a similar fate (dying young). There's a reason so many children in fairy tales lose their mothers—it's one of the scariest prospects for anyone to consider. And we'd be going right to the heart of these vulnerable people for a project about mothers!

Michelle knew her people, though, and was ready to guide them through writing and bearing witness for one another. She also wanted the writers to have their own space to document their journey in a written reflection separate from the story—another new thing.

As I said, the safety of the *My Mother's Story* experience has lain in the fact that it had decidedly not been about the writer's emotional journey—there's a phrase that comes up often in our writing labs: it's not about you! It takes effort for most people to stop thinking about themselves and to see their mothers as something other than their perfect or failed caregivers. However, I could see for *Gone Too Soon* that recording changing thoughts and feelings might be useful for the writers and I'll admit I was curious to know what they discovered. Many authors had talked of a "transformation", so maybe it would be a good thing to also have this documented.

The idea that clinched the deal was when Michelle mentioned she believed this collection could be a resource for people who were facing situations like these—children and adults, dealing with grief—to know they are not alone. It reminded me of a conversation I overheard in the early days of the project before one of our staged readings. An actor, veteran of six shows, whose mother died of alcoholism, told a newbie whose mother suffered abuse, "Don't be afraid of your story. You'll see—when you tell it you can feel the people out there who went through the same thing you did, or the same thing your mother did, and when you tell your story, you release them."

May you feel release from your story through reading ours. They are rich. Like a box of chocolates, you could consume them all in one sitting, but there's great value in savouring them one at a time. And may you find the courage to write your mother's story now.

Marilyn

Marilyn Norry
Editor & Founder of *My Mother's Story*
New Westminster, BC
March 13, 2022

PREFACE

It was in spring of 2014 when I found myself in a workshop called "The Story of Mother." The facilitator opened the session with an exercise designed to stimulate memories of our mothers with probing inquiries that related to the power of story.

I stared at the questions on the handout. I did not know the answers to the first two, and I was not sure I even understood the third. After a few minutes, the spaces in my worksheet were blank, blank, and blank.

I glanced discreetly at the laps of other attendees in the chairs surrounding me. These women were either deep in thought or had copious amounts of notes, while I seemingly had no memories about my mother, her kindness, or any true wisdom she may have conveyed. I reflected on the memories I *did* have, which all seemed to revolve around mother-daughter disagreements, getting in trouble, being reprimanded, or sent to my room to "think about my behaviour."

I knew in my soul there were so many more good things about my mom and my relationship with her; cherished moments worth capturing. So, why couldn't I remember them? It occurred to me in that moment that I didn't even know Mom's favourite colour or flower, let alone who she truly was as a woman or what her hopes and dreams may have been.

In the next exercise, we were asked to write down three things we learned from our mother. Okay, this seemed easier. Even though I was not yet a tween when Mom died, I must have picked up a thing or two.

I could hear the lead of pencils scribing words around me. I had to write *something*. But what had I learned from my mother? Deep breath…

1. Take good care of your skin (Mom had gorgeous, flawless skin)
2. Be home before the streetlights turn on, and I don't know…
3. Don't die?

I repositioned my arm to try to cover my relatively empty page. While this particular exercise made me feel like an underachiever, in the grief and bereavement world, I felt I had been working on things for quite a while. I had sought out therapy in my early twenties and had continued with professional support on-and-off over the years. I had read anything I could get my hands on relating to loss and grief, from the personal experiences of others in memoir, to empirical research and academic studies on the impacts of grief.

At age 46; my loss had been 35 years ago. I'd had time to reflect, and even to write about some of these reflections. I thought I was getting a better handle on loss and the cascade of potential emotional, physical, behavioural, spiritual, and family dynamic impacts that may affect the bereaved. But even with all this knowledge, I still either knew or remembered very little about my mom and who she was as a woman while she lived.

At the end of the session, I approached the workshop facilitator to ask her how, specifically, she got her memories back. She was far younger than I was when she had been separated from her natural mother and had also lost her adoptive one—a double maternal loss—yet she shared a deep pool of memories in vivid detail in her work. She had mentioned intensive meditation and hypno-regression therapy and I was keen to learn more.

"The first step, Michelle, is to surrender," she said. "Surrender to all that you might find, and to everything that is possible. That might sound easy, but believe me, it is the hardest thing you will ever do. You need to let go."

Although I was not completely sure what "surrendering" meant, leaning into an exploratory path with purpose and passion sounded good. Embarking on a journey of re-discovery and re-connection, even better. I acknowledged in that very moment that my identity—and my story—was inextricably linked to my mother's story.

I pledged on that day to surrender; to a newfound commitment to finding the answers to these questions; to finding out more about who Mom was as a living woman and not just one who died; to connecting with her presence, as opposed to still sometimes reeling from her absence; to finding that part of me and sense of self that I had lost; to finding my Mom; to *finding* Florence.

It was nine months later that *My Mother's Story* would find me…

After the 2014 Story of Mother workshop, I kept my pledge. I did embark on a new healing pilgrimage—a quest that involved throwing a *lot* of stuff against the wall to see what might stick; choosing a path that included both conventional and unconventional methods. I continued with counselling sessions and journaling, but I also surrendered to a wilder world of possibilities for the first time, including hypno-regression therapy, reiki practitioners, shamans, and psychic mediums. Alongside these new forms of exploration, I read more loss and grief memoirs and self-help books, attended grief workshops and retreats, and formed a support group for women who experienced early mother loss, called Wildflower. I travelled to places Mom either had been or wanted to go in the attempt to conjure her essence. I followed every bread crumb the universe sent me to find out more about my mother, Florence.

These were all helpful in a variety of ways and added a nuanced perspective to my healing. However, I could not help but feel that it was all still very much focused on *me* and did not quite access some of what I specifically wanted to learn about Mom.

Serendipitously—or via the law of attraction—I was introduced to *My Mother's Story* in early 2015 by a woman who would become one of our anthology authors, Christine Norris. My first writing 'lab' was with an all-female group at the North Vancouver public library. Our chairs were arranged in a talking circle, akin to ancient methods of sharing oral history, with Marilyn Norry—the charismatic founder and group leader—as our focal point, our fire.

Marilyn spoke about the project and its roots, explained the writing 'recipe', and led us through writing exercises designed to stimulate memory and capture those details on the page. The latter part of the lab was for reading full stories or excerpts of work out loud.

I listened to other authors who had detail-laden descriptions of mothers who were still very much alive, or who had passed in their 80s or 90s. They had shared a lifetime of lived experiences with their moms or had the ability to sit with her and ask questions directly. Comparing this to my sparse and uncertain 11-year-old memories, with no interviewee and lack of others in my life who were keen to revisit the past, was incredibly intimidating. All I could think was, *I can't do this. There is NO way I can write this.*

It was 2014 déjà vu.

But I did do it. It took me six months, and with Marilyn's patience, guidance, and the gentle support of the other motivating and welcoming authors in the labs, I was able to research, piece together, and upload "The Story of Florence" to the My Mother's Story online archive.

What struck me the most about *My Mother's Story* was the awareness of how powerfully it transported me out of my head for the first time on my healing journey—close to thirty-five years into it. The nature of the writing template made the impacts of *my* loss, *my* longing, and *my* lack ineligible to write about. So, I didn't.

These ground rules directed me to researching the facts of my mother's life, and with this new knowledge also came a new sense of connection and belonging. At the end of this process, foreign feelings like peace and ease emerged, and began to fill the section of my heart that had only known a long relationship with sadness and angst. A weight had been lifted, and I recognized the power of *My Mother's Story* as a way to re-frame the narrative of loss and as a potential broader healing tool.

I was so compelled by the impact of its cathartic and healing properties that I became Marilyn's first *My Mother's Story* facilitator. Between late 2015 and 2020, I ran *My Mother's Story* workshops; mostly for Wildflower and sometimes for mixed groups, including participants with living mothers. The continued experiences of 'finding' mothers—whether it be through unearthing new information or connecting with what had been lost—was equally powerful and repeatedly profound.

During this time, I became increasingly prepared to expand this important work further; my confidence having been lifted through writing my own mother's story. I began adding more resources to my toolkit. In addition to spending much of my day job writing and editing, my 'surrender journey' led me to expressive writing credentials, facilitating loss and grief journaling groups of my own curriculum design at a local hospice, and becoming a Registered Therapeutic Counsellor.

It was in early 2021 when the idea of *Gone Too Soon* was born. I proposed the creation of a new anthology to Marilyn with a specific theme; to have stories of early mother loss bound as a collection for use as a potential healing resource. It would be in keeping with the other *My Mother's Story* anthologies, telling the extraordinary stories of ordinary women; bringing focus to the lives they did have, albeit far too short.

As I reflect back on 2014, I can see more clearly how the "surrender" and "you need to let go," guidance unfolded over time. It meant yielding to the process, even if I was not sure precisely where it would lead. It meant accepting that there was still work to do, despite what I thought I knew, and the persistent social expectation that grief is somehow time bound and I should have been 'over it' by then. It meant letting go of the idea that my *only* option was to mourn or feel an ongoing undercurrent of lack and longing, which was perhaps holding me back from living a fuller life. It meant opening my mind to the possibility that additional—and even opposing—emotions surrounding significant loss could co-exist with grief. I had become so accustomed to sadness being my only tether to connection; it was through this process I learned that it is not a betrayal of that connection to also to feel joy when thinking about Mom.

There is naturally renewed sadness and perhaps even new pain when revisiting early mother loss. There is no escaping it, and this is why it takes a tremendous amount of strength and courage to embark on this project. Clearly, the entire notion of *Gone Too Soon* is fundamentally sorrowful. However, after writing these stories, the authors reveal an array of overarching outcomes that have been many, many things besides sad.

Through tracing and sharing the fullness of the lives our mothers did have as well as revealing portions of our journey and the variety of ways in which we 'came out the other side' of our grief, we found a collective space that has been comforting and uplifting.

The contributors to this anthology envision this collection as a potential healing companion to an audience seeking bereavement tools in a broad sense, as well as more specifically within the community of those who have experienced early mother loss. We hope all of our readers find these robust stories and authentic author reflections as poignant, resilient, and inspiring as we do.

Michelle

Michelle Hohn, MA, RTC
Editor & Contributing Author
Nanoose Bay, BC
March 13, 2022

INTRODUCTION

Write the story of your mother's life
—just the facts from beginning to end—
in less than 2,000 words,
where you are just a footnote.

When you are finished, and when you are ready,
read your story out loud to at least one person.

-Marilyn Norry
My Mother's Story: The Originals

This is the *My Mother's Story* writing template. It seems straightforward enough. However, it is actually somewhere between complicated and downright daunting if you are considering taking this on as an adult who was bereaved in childhood.

Gone Too Soon is a themed anthology—a courageous collection of stories using the *My Mother's Story* template—written by adults who experienced the loss of their mother in childhood or adolescence. This book offers the rich, lived experiences of twenty mothers and their twenty bereaved children—eighteen women and two men, ranging in age from thirty to seventy-six, and residing in four nations around the globe (Canada, the United States, the United Kingdom and South Korea).

Because the loss of their mothers was many years—or more likely decades—ago, and with such little time spent with them, the *Gone Too Soon* authors faced the immense challenge of piecing together their stories with no interviewee, using scant or non-existent memories, scouring attics or crawl spaces for photos, reaching out to the few (and potentially reluctant or resistant) family and friends who were still alive or available for discussions, in the attempt to trace a life lived.

They did all this while continuing to process an evaporating footprint and sorrowful ending on a timeline that, from a child's perspective, was unknown, foggy, or even purposefully shrouded in secrecy. This task embodied an enormous amount of emotional heavy lifting in addition to the practical impossibilities of finding answers to certain questions.

That said, the *My Mothers Story* model provides the opportunity to explore a painful childhood event from a different perspective—an adult perspective—reframing the narrative surrounding the event, and thus restructuring and re-wiring the thoughts previously associated with the event. This is critically important because many bereaved young are developmentally unable to fully grieve, which tends to embargo further processing until later in life—and at times, not at all. Adults bereaved in childhood thus potentially remain in a state of grief for longer or have an increased propensity towards developing unresolved grief.

Loss is an endemic aspect of the human condition and touches everyone at some point in their lives. The total number of parentally bereaved children and youth is not known, nor is it precise—these statistics are not systematically gathered, consistently tracked, or well documented—however, these estimates help demonstrate how prevalent this specific niche of the loss and grief demographic is:

- Canada (2016): Just over 7%—or an estimated 1 in 14 children—will experience the loss of a parent or sibling before they reach the age of 18. This equates to approximately 40,000 children per year losing a family member who was living in their home (Children and Youth Grief Network).
- United Kingdom (2011): 1 in 20 (approximately 4.7%) of young people will have experienced the death of one or both parents before age 16 (Childhood Bereavement Network).
- The United States (2015-2019): Approximately 3.9% (or 1 in 26) children experienced the loss of a parent or sibling before age 18; totalling over 2.85M children. According to the Childhood Bereavement Estimation Model (2021), 5.3 million (1 in 14), children in the U.S. are projected to experience the death of a parent or sibling before they reach the age of 18 (Judi's House / The Jag Institute).

These figures—even where outdated or incomplete—reveal a conservative, yet significant, estimate of the number of children who lose one or both of their parents before reaching adulthood. When non-death-related forms of loss are factored in, such as absence from separation and divorce, substance use, mental illness, or deployment, and taking into consideration expected adjustments to accommodate recent deaths associated with the Covid-19 global pandemic, children coping with loss could conceivably shift to an unwieldy or overwhelming segment of the grieving population.

If you are drawn to this book, you may have personally experienced mother loss (perhaps at a young age) and may very well be feeling alone in your grief. Perhaps your mother is still living, but you have felt other losses, and wish to understand more about the direct experience of others. You may be seeking resources to support someone you know in their loss and grief. Maybe you have not yet had a significant loss in your life, and wish to learn more about the bereavement process in general. Or, you may be familiar with the other *My Mother's Story* anthologies or the online archive and are keen to read the next series of extraordinary stories about ordinary women.

In addition to the stories themselves, readers will witness the benefits and positive outcomes of the expressive writing and journal therapy techniques that were intentionally embedded into the *Gone Too Soon* author experience.

Going beyond simple journaling or storytelling, this work included a focus on specific expression surrounding stressful or traumatic life events to understand, process, and integrate thoughts and emotions (Pennebaker, 2004 & 2016), and involved the therapeutic use of journaling exercises and reflective writing prompts to facilitate awareness and improvements to mental, emotional, physical, and spiritual health and wellbeing (Adams, 1990).

It is possible for readers to travel the path of each author—from a place where stories were silenced and painful emotions were held back, to a destination of resplendent letting go and surrendering that unfolds in unique ways in the life of each mother and in every reflection piece.

This blend of biography (honouring and celebrating the life of the deceased), and author reflective essay (revealing authentic elements of the journey of the bereaved), from twenty different perspectives on early mother loss, bound in one book is, to our knowledge, an original format. For this reason, we believe *Gone Too Soon* may be a unique resource and contribution to, the loss, grief, and bereavement field. These anthology authors learned together that the focus on mother and author together invited connection and evoked healing.

Readers may find other ways in which this book is inspirational or useful. That this is more than grief work; it is soul work, existential work, which speaks to us all. As psychotherapist and contributing author Mandy Gosling says, "Grief work is not done all in one go." (www.abcgrief.co.uk) There can be common misconceptions that it should be, rather than folding grief into the layers of our existence. The *My Mother's Story* concept is also flexible and extends far beyond writing about 'mother'—the protagonist of each story could just as easily be father, grandmother, grandfather, sibling, child, dear friend, or beloved animal companion. The healing possibilities are varied and vast.

How Gone Too Soon Came Together

With approval to move forward with the *Gone Too Soon* themed anthology concept, in early 2021 a network of people were contacted who had either directly experienced mother loss in childhood or adolescence, or those who might be in a position to help get word out. This included the Wildflower membership base, fellow expressive writing/Center for Journal Therapy classmates, and counselling/therapist peers.

The *Gone Too Soon* writing experience was presented not only as a storytelling and publication opportunity, but was intentionally positioned as having the potential to act as a loss and grief healing tool. This was layered with the objective of the original vision of *My Mother's Story*; namely the documentation of the female experience in women's history.

Author workshops and subsequent follow-up sessions—where authors read full stories or excerpts of their work out loud—took place from March to November 2021. All interaction and content delivery were conducted online, partially due to the Covid-19 pandemic, but also to accommodate the international nature and time zones of the participants.

The *My Mother's Story* workshop model was utilized for the author's engagement, writing, and sharing process. Writing exercises included some of the time-tested initiative techniques to begin to map out a chronological timeline for a story and to access memories. Topic-specific adjustments were made to guided meditations and new writing exercises containing journal therapy techniques were introduced, including: the Character Sketch, Captured Moments, the Unsent Letter, Perspectives, and the Alpha-Poem (Adams, 1990).

In addition to the story of their mother, each author was given the opportunity to craft a reflection piece. This permitted a new space to share impressions of their subjective experience as they moved through this process, articulating how it may have fit within the larger arc of their grief or may have contributed to their healing journey.

It was this autobiographical and altruistic nature of the reflection piece that turned out to be the most motivating factor for author participation in the collection—*despite* how difficult they may have anticipated it might be to write their mother's story. The ability to contribute to a potentially helpful resource for those seeking one—something many of us wish we had when we were feeling alone in our grief—was incredibly inspiring. Individuals who may have been hesitant to write in the past became intrigued by how writing in the act of service could be a powerful gift.

This author group was also encouraged to disclose when they *did not* have information or the answers to questions—particularly details that might seem obvious or easy to obtain by others who are not early bereaved—and to embed outstanding queries into the work and share this uncertainty with readers. Varying degrees of unknown-and-no-way-to-find-out was a repeating thread within the author tapestries and there was a desire to reflect this haunting nuance in the storytelling.

While counsellor-facilitated, the writing workshops and follow-up sessions were not structured as counselling or process groups. That said, group dynamics intrinsically provided the venue for "therapeutic factors" to emerge as well as corresponding positive outcomes that may promote healing, including the imparting of information, universality (the comfort that one is not alone), altruism (reciprocal giving and receiving), the installation of hope (witnessing healing 'progress' of others), catharsis, and group cohesiveness (Yalom, 2005). The gatherings provided a space for participants to share their private pain and perspectives, normalize feelings, validate experiences, empathize with other group members, about grief, loss, and other difficult life issues that could emerge, as well as bear witness to the women being honoured in stories.

Author Group Experiences

Shared Emotions

Over and above the writing exercises and overall instruction, the *Gone Too Soon* author workshop sessions intentionally curated a safe and contained space for sharing a range of challenging emotions. Authors had the option of exploring emerging emotions in group, or more fully in private within the individual editing sessions with the counsellor-facilitator. In addition to expressions of heartache, sadness, and feelings of being disconnected or an aloneness in grief and loss related pain, some of the more prevalent feelings at the beginning of the process included:

- Anxiety—a resistance to looking back; a hesitancy to re-open old wounds and undoubtedly re-visit pain, tentativeness about 'rocking the family boat' by opening-up the topic with new rounds of questions.
- Fear—of feeling, of increasing pain, and of the unexpected.

There was already so much that was unknown. What if something even more painful was uncovered? Of failure; what if I cannot do this? What if I get my mother's story 'wrong?'

- Excitement—a chance to be heard, a way for their mother to be known, a force that allowed difficult emotions to transform and kept author momentum strong.
- Anger—at feeling 'ripped off' or short-changed for losing mothers young; at choices our mothers may have made that we did not—or maybe still do not—understand, at a system that failed them, at ourselves for failing memories.
- Guilt—for not knowing more; for not asking our mothers more, for not being as interested in her life as we 'should have been,' not being physically present in her time of need—regardless of how young or what developmental stage we would have been and how unrealistic those capabilities might be.
- Shame—feelings of 'less than,' of being different through being deprived of the full experience of being mothered/ feeling unmothered. In some cases, shame or embarrassment in *how* she passed.

As the work progressed, these predominantly difficult and uncomfortable emotions, while initially intensifying in nature, began to subside and/or shift and transform to feelings such as joy, peace, and gratitude. These positive and comforting additions tended to appear alongside feelings of increased belonging and connection—which are generously documented within the reflection pieces. Authors collectively arrived at a new destination where the co-existence of both sadness and joy relating to grief could be experienced simultaneously.

The author expressions at the end of the process—feelings of connection, belonging, gratitude, and resilience—are a remarkable manifestation of ritual, remembrance, and represent the tangible formation of a continuing bond, (Klass, Sliverman, & Nickman,

1996), and finding an enduring connection and way to remember the deceased, while simultaneously moving forward with life, with optimism for the future (Worden, 2018).

Shared Themes Within the Writing

Once the mother stories and author reflections were complete and compiled, there were patterns of meaning and resonating themes noted throughout the lived experiences, some of which included:

- The paradigm shift from the common narrative of *loss and impact from loss* prior to this work—which was how mothers died, and how old they/we were at the time they passed—to *who these women were, what they valued, and how they lived.* Changing the narrative from a mother's absence to feeling her presence.

- The validation of participating in a process where cultivating memory begets more memory. Authors spoke or wrote of an increase in real memories as well as an increase in comfort from felt experiences.

- An increased sense of self through newfound connection with Mom; knowing one's place in the world, a feeling of belonging, a connection with mother, but also a transgenerational bond—learning about *her* mother and father as well. A quietening of the question "I don't know my mother, so who am I?" This transformational process, integrated the known and the unknown parts of self, became healing and joyful (Gosling, 2016).

- The creative use of *My Mother's Story* as a voice. Several authors spoke to the appeal of giving their mother a voice through this work as well as utilizing the structure for direct communication with their mothers; the use of the 'unsent letter', the second person point of view/writing to her, or in two instances, writing 'as' her.

- An unexpected amount of intergenerational early loss was uncovered in the story-telling process. Several mothers in the stories also experienced loss in childhood or adolescence.

- Authors pondering whether early life stresses or trauma experienced by their mothers may have been a catalyst for disease or terminal illness in later life—a wondering about causal links.
- The consistent computation of time using relational math— using the age of mother at the time of her passing, and how many 'years since' as a way to situate in, and measure time. This is perhaps more objectively calculated after this work, as opposed to carrying intense ache in those numbers.
- A sense of surprise when first feeling the co-existence of emotion. A sense of comfort or joy simultaneously with grief—almost wonder—at the realization of the ability to hold both, and integrate celebrating into the remembering and honouring process.

My Mother's Story is a powerful and purposive act of ritual and remembrance. The *Gone Too Soon* method invited this bereaved-in-childhood group of authors to a landscape where sense and meaning-making reside, providing an additional, and much-needed tool to access the spirit of those who are no longer with us.

The anthology authors brought with them their intelligence, experience, vulnerability, creativity, honesty, and courage in their desire to honour their mothers. They leaned into genuine empathy and compassion to share their experience with others on the grieving continuum. If readers could be shown one successful method of moving along that continuum from 'there to here'—perhaps they can do it too.

These twenty stories—individual beams of light forming one beacon—illuminate a belief that the *My Mother's Story* model is a powerful invitation to facilitate ongoing conversations surrounding loss. The published works and online archive—through the conduit of storytelling—ensure that we do not forget the extraordinary lives of ordinary women. And, the *Gone Too Soon* collection compels us to consider that, while perhaps difficult, asking questions surrounding life's challenges brings meaning, and contributes to individual journeys of self-discovery and healing.

1 | Linda Higgins' Story of Anne

My mom was more than a mother; she was my best friend. Her funeral was at the United Church in Whitehorse, Yukon. My dad and I sat in the front row along with aunts, uncles, and my granny. Many friends and colleagues, who I did not know, filled the church and accompanied us to a graveside ceremony, followed by a reception at our home. The year was 1986, I was thirteen years old and in shock, although I did not know it at the time. I felt like I was watching the entire scene from a distance, unable to feel or understand.

Anne Kulchysky was born on December 22, 1938, on a farm near Gronlid, Saskatchewan. Her parents, Fedora Moskal and Mykola Kulchysky, were both immigrants from Ukraine, who travelled to Canada in 1910 and 1913, respectively. They married in 1920 and proudly farmed their quarter section of land.

Anne was the youngest child of eight, all of whom were born on the farm. Her siblings, from oldest to youngest, were Mary, John, Katherine, Walter, Millie, Stephen, and Pauline. Stephen died within the first year of his life. Mary was an invalid from a farm accident and died at 30 years of age.

Anne Kulchysky was baptized at St. Mary's Ukrainian Orthodox Church on March 9, 1939. She first learned to speak Ukrainian and later English from her siblings and at school.

Anne loved animals. The earliest photo of Anne showed her barefoot in a dress with the family dog Sport. She had a pet chicken with a red stripe painted on its head and rode the family horse, King, back and forth to school, often with friends or neighbours on the back. In fact, all of Anne's early pictures included animals.

She helped with farm chores and was a tomboy. She played hockey and baseball with her pals from grade and middle schools, both of which were one-room farm schools. Anne completed grade 10 and then moved to Prince Albert, where she completed secretarial courses at Prince Albert Business College.

Anne loved music and became a proud member of the Elvis Presley fan club in 1957. She loved country and western music artists such as Johnny Cash, Patsy Cline, and Buck Owens. She loved everything country and western, from comics to movies.

She moved to Edmonton around 1958, where her siblings Pauline and Walter lived and worked as a telephone operator for Alberta Government Telephones.

In November 1963, Anne went on a Mexican holiday with her good friend, Helen. From the inscriptions on several black and white photographs, they had a fun time exploring, seeing bullfights, meeting boys and dancing to a mariachi band. She had several friends and went on picnics and to parties, where she drank one Tia Maria and Cream.

Anne often drove to visit her parents, who lived with her brother John and his wife Audrey, on the family farm. Two families in a farmhouse with two small children was a difficult situation, which was remedied when, in 1965, Anne bought her parents a small house in the hamlet of Gronlid. She also bought a stove and furnace for the house. The house was rustic, without running water, but it was their own cozy home.

In 1968, Anne had a disagreement with her brother, Walter. Over what, she never shared with her future husband or daughter, but the event precipitated her leaving Edmonton. Anne and her girlfriend Avril, who also quit her job with Alberta Government Telephones, got in Anne's new Plymouth Fury and drove 2,152 km on the Alaska Highway—all the way to the Yukon Territory. They settled in Haines Junction.

Anne waitressed at the Kluane Park Inn near Whitehorse. John Higgins was travelling the highway for his job with the Department of Public Works and, over lunch in the café, saw Anne for the first time. He was instantly attracted to her. In the summer, Anne moved to Whitehorse and rented a room from people she knew from Saskatoon. She found another job as a toll operator, this time with Canadian National Telecommunications.

Anne and John were formally introduced on August 9, 1970, through mutual friends. They were getting to know each other, and John mentioned that he might drive over the Top of the World Highway into Dawson City for Discovery Day Celebrations. Anne was also thinking about going to Discovery Days and John hoped they would see each other there.

Two weeks later, Anne was walking down one of Dawson's boardwalks and ran into John. They ate supper together and explored the town, which was full of visitors. Since there were no available accommodations, Anne and John had to sleep in Anne's Plymouth Fury.

That was it; they started going together from then on. She moved into John's house, and they became a 'Yukon Couple', but she never told her parents about it. She discovered on May 17, 1972, that she was pregnant and upon hearing the news, John asked Anne to marry him. After a 48-hour engagement, they married at the Whitehorse Courthouse in a civil ceremony with two of their closest friends standing up for them, Arnold and Della Jeffers.

Anne wore a white dress with a gauzy white wrap decorated with light brown polka dots, a red corsage, white gloves, and high heels. She had short brown hair and cat eye glasses. They later celebrated at the 202 Club, the best steak house in town.

Anne quit her job as an operator and Linda Ann Higgins, the light of Anne's life, was born on December 28, 1972, at Whitehorse General Hospital. She was a healthy baby girl, weighting 6 pounds and 4.5 ounces.

John worked various jobs—on road construction crews—for Finning Tractor, and as a heavy equipment mechanic in addition to running his own companies. Anne stayed home and took care of Linda, ran the household, and was a partner in the family businesses. Anne turned the entire back yard into a garden with berry and rhubarb patches and row upon row of vegetables. She carefully weeded and tended the garden and preserved the fruits of her labour for the winter.

Anne wanted to have more children and became pregnant three years after Linda was born. Tragically, there were complications about seven months into her pregnancy, and she delivered a stillborn girl. Anne was devastated and decided not to try for any more children. Baby Higgins was buried on July 18, 1975, at Grey Mountain Cemetery.

When Linda was old enough, Anne walked her to preschool, which was about two blocks from home. Linda was a shy child, so Anne would stay until Linda felt comfortable. She would return to walk her home and continued to do so when Linda went to Selkirk Street Elementary School.

Anne was devoted to her daughter and all her after-school activities. She bought Linda a green tricycle to ride until she graduated to a green two-wheel bike. Anne patiently held the seat until Linda learned how to ride. Anne also took Linda to swimming lessons, waiting at the bottom of the slide, promising to catch her as soon as she touched the water. Anne watched all her figure skating practices and sewed all of her ice carnival costumes.

At Christmas, Anne honoured her Ukrainian roots by putting a star and a straw-filled manger under the dining room table. She would stay up late making fruit salad, cucumber mould, and preparing Christmas dinner. She would always have a bath on Christmas Eve, hoping Linda would fall asleep so she could fill stockings and put out Santa's presents. Anne would put mixed nuts and Christmas oranges in stockings and always made sure there were plenty of presents under the tree.

Around 1977, Anne was in the bathtub when she discovered a lump in her breast. She was diagnosed with breast cancer and had a partial mastectomy, followed by chemotherapy. During her illness, it was the first time Linda was cared for by a babysitter. Anne was very sick and, despite having a subsequent complete mastectomy, she never felt quite right afterwards. She said to her husband, "I will never take chemotherapy again; I would die first."

John lost his job at Finning Tractor during a recession in 1982, but found work in Prince Rupert at Foundation Skanska building grain silos. Anne did not want to move there because of some previous family history, so John rented an apartment while Linda and Anne stayed in Whitehorse.

Anne's father had worked in the logging industry in Prince Rupert in the 1940s to augment his farm finances, but Anne would shut down whenever John asked her any questions about the experience.

In the summers, Anne and Linda often travelled to Gronlid in the old Plymouth Fury. Anne would do chores like repainting the outside of the house. She would give her mother a pedicure, set her hair in pin curls, and dye her sister Katherine's hair. The majority of the town was Ukrainian, and Anne felt at home there.

Anne eventually went back to work as a telephone operator at Northwestel. She enjoyed her independence and earning her own money. Linda was not keen on being left alone, often insisting on going with Anne and was once caught in the work bathroom. Then she waited in the car and finally started waiting on her own at home. One time, Linda found some candles above the fridge and lit them out of curiosity. Anne was terrified and furious, which scared Linda so badly she never played with candles again.

Whenever the Edmonton Oilers were on television, Anne watched while crocheting delicate dollies and warm afghans. She also learned to knit gloves and made several pairs. She loved to watch the Oilers, especially when Wayne Gretzky led the team to several Stanley Cup victories. If the Oilers were not on, she watched *The Tommy Hunter Show* or *Dallas*.

In July 1985, Anne and Linda drove to Saskatchewan for the wedding of her niece, Sonia. On the way back, twelve-year-old Linda occasionally drove, feeling proud and grown-up, but it was likely because Anne was not feeling well. Anne had admitted to her brother John that this would likely be her last visit to the farm.

The cancer had progressed, but this time Anne did not tell her husband. She kept it to herself because she did not want to have chemotherapy again. John came home from an extended work trip and expressed concern about how gingerly Anne was walking. The truth finally came out, but despite her hesitation, John managed to convince Anne to see a new specialist and she flew to Vancouver the next day.

Anne spent Christmas in the hospital with her husband and daughter. There were many tears when they left so Linda could return to school. Anne came back to Whitehorse in February and went straight to Whitehorse General Hospital, where she died on May 24, 1986.

John and Linda bought Anne a rose-coloured headstone engraved with wheat stocks and a colt, representing her Saskatchewan farm roots, her love of horses and her favourite colour. She was laid to rest beside Baby Girl Higgins at Grey Mountain Cemetery.

My mom left a legacy of independence and adventure. She was kind to people and animals alike: my dad said my mother was the kindest person he had ever met. She was a private woman who was loyal and hard working. She loved me fiercely and gave me the foundation to become the strong woman I am today.

ANNE AND JOHN, 1972, WHITEHORSE, YUKON

Author Reflection - Linda Higgins
Parksville, BC, Canada

When I began to write my mother's story, the rich story of Anne began to unfold. I was able to see her life through my adult eyes, and better understand her decisions and personality. I love how fearless and adventurous she was, and without this writing exercise, I wouldn't have been able to experience some of her adventures.

Being an adult who experienced early mother loss, I would desperately like to go back in time and have an adult conversation with my mother. I would like to know if she is proud of me, why she moved to the Yukon, what her parents' emigration experience was like, her hopes and dreams for me, and even how she was able to make her dumplings so fluffy. What I wouldn't give to be able to call her and talk about anything, and nothing at all.

Surprisingly, the other gift of this storytelling experience was a stronger relationship with my father. When I was nearing a completed and more polished final draft, I shared my mother's story with my dad. I was nervous about his reaction, but I wanted his approval and permission. Not only was he supportive and engaged, he was willing and able to give me new information about my mom and their life together.

We never talked much about her death, maybe because we weren't able to talk about our feelings at that time. Thankfully, my writing and his reading my mother's story gave us the opportunity to explore our feelings. It was the catalyst that enabled me to clearly see how deeply he loved my mother, which I was unable to appreciate earlier.

My dad gave me the second last line of my story, which describes my mom's kindness: he said my mother was "the kindest person he ever met." That was a precious gift, and I am profoundly grateful for how he opened up to me in a way he never had before. In that moment, I was able to deepen my understanding of him and their relationship. In forgiving him, I was also able to forgive myself and release the anger and some of the sadness I have been carrying around with me for so long.

Thirty-five years have passed since my mother's death, and although I am not able to go back and talk with my mom, I have more empathy and grace, and I feel her presence all around me.

2 | Susan Teresa Bocchinfuso's Story of Adele

I remember walking around the stacks of newspapers. There were so many. Everywhere. Under the coffee table, in piles around the house, on top of the kitchen table, and spilling out of bookshelves. I was around seven years old when I noticed that our house had an abnormal level of mess and chaos, and it seemed the amount of paper was a constantly expanding field. Only as an adult looking through the lens of my mother's story can I see the order in the chaos she created.

Adelaide ("Adele") Dmytrow was born in Radway, Alberta, on October 4, 1937. Her parents, Fred and Katie (nee Chornohous), immigrated to Canada from the Ukraine and had two children—Adele and her brother Alexander. They tried their best to settle into a new country with a new language, customs, and culture, and taught their children to be proud of their Ukrainian heritage.

Adele's family struggled. Life as settlers was physically demanding, and Fred learned fast that he would have to find another way to make a living. He started a grocery store that failed, then tried a café that also failed, and eventually got into real estate. He bought a hotel—his business sense having finally paid off—and he became financially successful. Personally, however, he struggled with stress. To cope, the occasional drink to settle the nerves turned into a regular affair. He died in 1953 when Adele was fifteen due to complications from alcoholism.

After she finished high school, Adele moved to Edmonton, which was a thriving metropolis compared to the small village where she grew up. Self-sufficiency and independence were values she held in high regard, and she knew from her parents' struggle that an education would be paramount in her finding a better life for herself. Adele completed a diploma in office management and started working for an insurance company. She was proud of her job and did it well. Despite her desire for self-reliance and self-sufficiency, she never learned how to drive until much later in her life.

Adele took the bus every morning to work. On one particular morning, her routine was interrupted by a man named Giuseppe, who pulled over at her bus stop to offer her a ride. Never in her right mind would she accept a ride from a stranger! She thought it was a one-off event, but every couple of days, he would return. And every time, she politely declined. Each time they engaged in some idle chit-chat, which soon turned into lengthy conversations. He was handsome, forward, and attentive. She was a brown-eyed beauty (it's no wonder she caught his eye) and he was one of the few people in her life who listened to her and paid her the attention she had been craving all these years. After weeks of these drive-by chats, she finally decided to accept a ride. Their courtship started, and they were engaged soon after.

It was a long engagement. Adele's mother, after many years struggling in her marriage with an alcoholic, had suffered a mental breakdown and was institutionalized. She died soon after by suicide. Adele's brother, Alexander, who had moved to the States and served in the military, felt that he should have a claim to the entire estate because he was a man and women didn't know how to manage money. They had a falling out and didn't speak for 20 years.

When Adele and Joseph (she never called him by his Italian name, Giuseppe) finally tied the knot in a small service in 1966 (Adele was 29), neither she nor her fiancé had any family present at their wedding. Joseph's family couldn't afford to fly over from Italy, and Adele was now alone.

Adele and her husband were both frugal and hard-working people. She knew how to manage money well and was very good at saving. They rented for a while and soon had enough money to buy their first home. From her work at the insurance company and the small inheritance she'd received from her mom, she set aside some funds to purchase rental properties. She also helped her husband start a business that would later become very successful. Like her father, Adele had a keen eye for real estate and enjoyed the thrill of making a deal. She eventually left her job at the insurance company to manage the rental properties.

In addition to her work, Adele also wanted to start a family. After ten years and multiple pregnancy losses, she finally became pregnant at 39. This was sometimes a source of social stigma for her, as she was acutely aware of her status as an 'older mother.' In 1976, her daughter Susan was born. Mom did want more children, but it just never worked out.

My mother never spoke about the death of her parents, her multiple pregnancy losses, or what it was like to be a parentless parent, although her actions spoke volumes. She channelled her personal trauma into being a hands-on, fully engaged mother. Tending my mental and physical well-being helped her navigate her unhappy and unhealthy marriage. My dad always said she found her voice after I was born. Her quiet and reserved personality changed as well, and a newfound confidence inspired my mom to learn how to drive. We didn't have a lot of money at the time, and her car was a lemon, but she was so proud of it and the independence that it brought her.

Although freshly baked cookies were never in her repertoire, we spent hours upon hours talking, drawing, dancing, reading, and delighting in each other's company. Her love was fierce, her laugh was infectious, and her hugs were out of this world. I remember all my friends gravitating towards her. Although she was by nature quite reserved and never wished to be the centre of attention, there would always be a subtle shift in the room whenever my mom entered. Things always seemed a bit lighter when she was around.

She was one of those people who would start a conversation with you and make you feel like you were the only person in the world. She had a knack for remembering that one mundane detail that you were sure no one else was paying attention to—but sure enough, my mom would remember it. And if it was important to you, she would ask you about it after weeks or months had gone by.

It was impossible to walk away from an interaction with her and not feel absolutely cared for.

In addition to caring for me, her other role was to manage the properties she and her husband owned. As a property owner, Adele wasn't very efficient. When she went to collect rent, she would end up chatting to people about what was happening in their lives. It took such a long time! Even though I was bored out of my mind as a child, I remember following her and picked up on the fact that people really loved talking to her. She always brought something: a gift if someone had a baby or a surprise cut in rent if someone was going through a hard time.

Mom was a free spirit and an independent thinker who liked to break the rules. One of my fondest memories was of her Sunday morning shopping trips. Dad was Catholic, but although they were married in the church, Mom was not a religious person. He would attend his own services in Italian, and on Sunday mornings, Mom would promise Dad that she would take me to church. I had no desire to go either, so she would drive us there, I would run up the stairs and dip my hands in holy water, do the sign of the cross, and pack myself back into the car. That way, we weren't lying if we were asked if we went to church! And off we would go to the mall to do some shopping and get some brunch.

Shopping was one of Mom's great pleasures, especially if she could find a great deal. If she found a pair of pants she liked, she would buy them in every available colour. Her pragmatic, yet fun-loving approach to life made for some interesting fashion choices. Bell-bottom pants in every colour of the rainbow and airy polyester blouses were her standard uniform. These were generally paired with stockings and open-toed sandals. I don't think she owned a pair of high heels, but she had a collection of clogs and other functional footwear that would rival the inventory of a small shoe store.

Mom and Dad's marriage was rocky at the best of times. My father's attentiveness and lack of patience in their first several years turned into possessive jealousy and fits of white-hot rage, which were brought on by the added pressures of parenthood. Mom's social circle started to dwindle, and none of her friendships survived. Rage morphed into full-on abuse. Hitting, shoving, and hair-pulling became a weekly occurrence. The injuries she sustained were never bad enough to land her in a hospital, but they were bad enough to break her spirit. Verbal assaults were a regular occurrence. These were much more effective at terrifying her into submission as they left no bruises or marks. It was around this time that she started to hoard papers everywhere. Our house was usually messy, but this brought it to another level entirely. So much mess.

One afternoon, after a particularly bad fight, I remember she had 'had enough' and got me dressed so we could go to the women's shelter. She was ready, and I was excited we were finally leaving. Living in fear was so exhausting for both of us. I will never forget the crestfallen look on her face when she told me the shelter was at capacity and we would have to try again another day. She lost her nerve to try again, but little did I know she had another plan, and that it involved the papers she hoarded.

Every month over the course of several years, my mom was secretly putting together our get-away money. When she went to collect rent from the tenants, she would skim off the top. She could get away with it because she did the books. What I thought was careless hoarding was our secret escape money hidden in plain sight! The newspapers contained cash—50s, 20s, and 100 dollar bills slipped between the pages. Her system was to highlight or fold the front page of the papers that had money. This was pure genius, as it was before the days of ATMs and before women could easily open their own bank accounts.

Sadly, we never got to leave together. My mom was diagnosed with Stage 4 cancer when she was 48. I was nine years old. When the cancer started, the abuse stopped. As there were no family or friends around and my dad worked out of town, Mom took me with her to most of her cancer treatments. She was given six months but managed to hang on for a full two years, which was a medical miracle in itself.

She died shortly after her 50th birthday. I cared for her as she was dying. We'd chat while she was getting a blood transfusion, or I would count the dots on the floor while I waited for her radiation therapy to finish. When she felt strong enough, we would have a post-chemo lunch ritual that never changed. She enjoyed having a familiar face around, and I know she wanted to maximize every bit of our time together.

Neither of us would have had it any other way.

ADELE, 1965

Author Reflection - Susan Teresa Bocchinfuso
Calgary, AB, Canada

What started as a very sad story about cancer, spousal abuse, and death turned out to be a turning point for me that I could not have ever imagined. My personal experience is tragic, but it is not at all unique. Whether your mom died 50 years ago or last week, our society needs better conversations surrounding grief—and this is what *My Mother's Story* and the workshopping groups did for me.

This process helped me take my heartbreak—which I have been quietly sitting with in the shadows for over 30 years—and understand it from a completely different perspective. People speak about the transformative power of grief: that had never resonated with me before, and I never really understood it. What I do understand is the fact that the loss of my mother will always be a part of my life. This is something I have struggled with for years. I have always wanted to process the pain and yet tuck it neatly back into a box so I don't need to deal with it.

Putting my mother's story down on paper illuminated the fact that tucking her experience back into the corner of my mind, only to be taken out again on milestones and random holidays, served no one in my life, especially me. It was as if she was dying a second time, but this time at my hand. Taking the hard lessons she learned and integrating them into my life is how I can—and will—honour my mother from now on. Instead of the memories weighing me down, her experience and the lessons she has taught me inform every possible dimension of my life.

But none of this would have been possible on my own. Being in the company of others who have experienced similar losses and could bear witness to her story and my pain were the salve to the wounds that needed to be reopened. And in reopening the wounds came more understanding, healing, and compassion, not only for my mother but also for me. This process has helped me appreciate that sometimes we complicate the simple facts.

Grief is about love. Even after death, love will always reign supreme.

3 | Tamara Mercer's Story of Marlene

Marlene Gertrude—my mother—was born August 3, 1932, in the town of Unity, Saskatchewan, to Beatrice Lola Janowsky and an unknown man. All I was told about my paternal grandfather was that he was the son of the owner of the car dealership in town and that he had been a "drinker and a wife beater." Beatrice was the youngest of a large family, and at eighteen, she was ill-prepared to deal with the situation, never mind motherhood. As a result, her family sent Beatrice and Marlene away to live with one of Beatrice's older sisters.

Those early years of my mother's life involved moving from one place to another, and eventually mother and daughter arrived in Vancouver, where Beatrice found a job working in a sewing factory. The two lived in tiny suites that had once been upstairs bedrooms in large houses, and my mother would later recall having many babysitters while Beatrice worked and went to business school.

Beatrice met William (Bill) Wilde in 1937. Bill worked in the interior decorating department of the Canadian National Railway, which owned several hotels, including the Hotel Vancouver, Chateau Lake Louise, and the Banff Springs Hotel in Alberta. Somehow, Bill convinced Beatrice to join him at his new posting at Banff Springs, where he was sure that he could get her work with her seamstress skills. Beatrice and Marlene arrived in Banff, where Bill found them a place to stay, and secured Beatrice a job in the interior decorating department, as he had promised.

My mother talked fondly of her time in Banff. She enjoyed the outdoor life, and she worshipped Bill. When my mother was six years old, Bill and Beatrice married on Christmas Eve, allowing the happy couple a one-day honeymoon on Christmas Day.

Afterwards, the new little family settled into a small rental house together.

Beatrice and Bill did not have any children together, but Bill treated Marlene like his own daughter. Eventually, the Wilde family moved back to Vancouver. Bill went to war, came back, and, after several moves, purchased a brand-new home in Burnaby, a suburb of Vancouver. Bill loved children and encouraged Marlene to bring her friends over, and as a young teen, the Wilde house was the place to be.

My mother was not a scholar, but she attended business college, and after graduating, she found a job with BC Electric, one of the province's main electrical providers. She met and married an electrician named Ken in 1951 when she was nineteen years old. One of my favourite pictures of my mother is a stunning black-and-white photo of her in a simple but elegant wedding gown.

The marriage to Ken was short-lived. By all accounts, it was an amicable split between two young people that had simply drifted apart. Newly single, my mother joined the BC Electric Social Club. This was where all the younger employees would get together after work for picnics, dances, and other social gatherings. My mother was very outgoing and personable. She had a curvy body and, coupled with her shiny dark wavy hair, brown eyes, and perfectly manicured nails, she stood out in the crowd. I can remember thinking that my mother looked like a blend of Elizabeth Taylor and Judy Garland.

My mother met my father while working at BC Electric. It was not love at first sight. She would often tell the story that he would walk by the typing pool, and all the girls would be 'oohing and aahing' at him. She said she "wanted to stick her foot out and watch him fall flat on his face." She felt he had an air of superiority about him and wasn't a fan. Somehow she got over that 'air of superiority' issue as the two started dating in 1953. Robert (Bob) Gordon Mercer had recently separated from his wife and was living at home with his parents. Bob's two sons from that marriage, Brian and Allan, lived with their mother, Barbara.

My father and mother dated for months and married in

November 1954. True to my mother's style, they invited their friends over to the Wilde's for a party. It was only when the guests arrived, they discovered they were at a wedding reception.

After saving for two years, my parents bought our family home in North Vancouver. 1960 Berkley Avenue was a brand, new house and to make ends meet, they had a roommate, a girl that my mother worked with. She would later become my godmother.

After five miscarriages and doctors' orders to stay in bed for most of the pregnancy, my mother gave birth to me, Tamara Denise Mercer, in September of 1960. My father had wanted a girl he could name after the popular Tammy movies of the 1960s.

Thirteen months later, my mother gave birth to premature twins; Michelle and Michael. At this time, twins were uncommon, and there was much fanfare about their arrival.

Those early years of motherhood were physically and mentally exhausting for my mother. This was a time before disposable diapers, plastic baby bottles, baby monitors, and many other modern conveniences young mothers enjoy today. She lived in suburbia without a car and no bus service; she was isolated and alone. The neighbouring mothers were in their 20s and happy to be housewives.

My mother was 30 years old and wanted to be anything but a housewife. She desperately wanted to return to work, have some independence, and her own money. My mother didn't do idle chit-chat well, and she certainly wasn't interested in Tupperware parties and gathering for tea with the other moms to discuss the latest daytime soap opera.

My mother's anxiety and unhappiness grew. Michael was a colicky baby, and his constant screaming was pushing my mother over the edge. She would often have outbursts of uncontrollable anger, followed by hours of crying. I remember feeling frightened of my mother and not knowing what to do. Although my father was, in retrospect, very helpful in the home, he was away five days a week. I think it was the long hours alone with three children that caused the first cracks in my mother's mental health.

My mother had her first stay in a psychiatric hospital when I was three. All I remember about the event was my Papa Wilde taking us to see her, and as we stood outside, she waved to us from her bedroom window. After she returned, my mother went on a vacation to the Cayman Islands. I do not know how my parents afforded such a luxury; we were told that she needed time away. I recall this time clearly because after my mother's return, she often played Caribbean Ska music on the record player.

It was after my mother's stay in the hospital that she started taking prescription drugs. I remember my father coming home every Friday night with a white bag from the drugstore. My mother's bedside table had a multitude of plastic bottles containing coloured pills. It was around this time she started drinking scotch and milk.

It is interesting how memories work. I can remember some like it was yesterday and others live in a fog. I remember when John F. Kennedy was assassinated. Why? Because my mother was ironing, I was playing on the living room floor, and the twins were in their respective playpens. The television was on, and suddenly my mother started crying. When I asked her what was wrong, she replied, "The President's been shot." I asked, "What's a President?"

My mother returned to work as a Girl Friday for Matsumoto Shipyard when I was seven and I, along with my brother and sister, officially became 'latchkey kids'. My mother seemed to enjoy her job, and her emotional outbursts lessened. However, she quit after a disagreement over time off. She then secured a position with BC Hydro, which was the new name of the power company in British Columbia, and where my father worked as the Manager of Accounts Payable.

My mother worked in the Purchasing Department, first as a clerk and then as a Work Leader. My mother working allowed our family to become members of the local Winter Club. In our pre-teen years, we played hockey, and our parents curled in various leagues. During the summer, when our parents were at work, we would pack a lunch and ride our bikes down to the Club to spend the day swimming.

Nana and Papa Wilde owned waterfront property on Salt Spring Island. They had purchased it in the early 1950s, intending to build their retirement home there one day. Together with my parents, they built a one-room cabin without the aid of electricity. To say the cabin was a labour of love would be an understatement. My mother so enjoyed her time at the cabin; I can vividly remember her sitting at the top of the path to the beach crying because she didn't want to go home.

In the late 1960s, Nana and Papa built their dream home as planned, moving the cabin to the other side of the property. Renovations to the cabin meant the children no longer slept on the porch but in the newly added bunk room.

In the early 1970s, our family started to unravel. My mother was acting more and more erratic, and she and my father fought constantly. The recurring episodes of depression, alternated with some bizarre behaviours such as prowling around the house at night, not sleeping, having wild ideas to redecorate or sell the house, or adopting a patient she met at the psychiatric hospital.

As time went on, things worsened. She did not seem to have a filter, blurting out thoughts or feelings to whoever would listen. On occasion, she would behave inappropriately, embarrassing the family.

There were many admissions to the psychiatric hospital. Each time she would come home happy, but she would soon dissolve into an angry, screaming, crying mess. Miraculously, she maintained her job. The flexible work schedule and robust sick leave plan concealed the true nature of her illness.

My high school existence was a nightmare, culminating on my graduation night with my drunk mother screaming, "Let me out!" and tumbling out of our moving car as we approached the high school entrance. Astonishingly, she was unhurt, but the stares of my classmates and averting eyes of their parents were seared into my memory as quickly as the redness to my face.

In 1980, my parents became empty nesters, and my mother's behaviour worsened. Labour Day weekend, my mother was on one of her 'benders' as we called them. She was drinking and taking pills. The whole neighbourhood heard her screaming out the window at my father as he worked in the garden. According to my father, he could not reason with her, and she finally went to bed in the early evening.

The following morning, my father entered the bedroom with my mother's tea tray as he had done over the last twenty years. Laying the tea tray down on her dresser, he went to wake her. That's when he knew. Empty pill bottles and a half glass of scotch told the story. Some would argue it was accidental, but I don't think so. She had a history of notes and wills on the nightstand.

There was no funeral, just a short obituary and few tears. Nobody used the word 'suicide.' In fact, nobody talked at all. My mother was cremated; her ashes scattered in the ocean in front of the property at Salt Spring. Pictures of her were boxed up and taken to the crawl space. My sister and I sent her clothes away. It was almost like she never existed. Life moved on, and she was seldom spoken of again.

MARLENE, 1951, BURNABY, BC

Author Reflection - Tamara Mercer
Fanny Bay, BC, Canada

When first introduced to the *My Mother's Story* project five years ago, I was hesitant. I'm the kind of person who believes the windshield is bigger than the rear-view mirror for a reason: I look forward to what's ahead and am far less concerned about what is behind me. I was also reluctant to involve myself in reliving or even reflecting on my mother's story. After all, most of her time on earth, as it related to me, was when I was a self-centred teenager. This skewed my view of my upbringing and my mother and her illness. It wasn't until I got older, matured, and experienced real life, as well as my own run-ins with depression, that any compassion for my mother and her situation emerged.

When I finally decided to put 'hands to keyboard', it gave me time to reflect more fully about my mother's circumstances, and that is when I became angry at a system that failed her; a system that allowed her an endless supply of prescription drugs when the doctors had to know she was also abusing alcohol. Through my new research and recollections, I have additional questions. It seemed to me the system put my mother into care, surrounded her with helpful, well-meaning nurses and doctors. She probably attended one-on-one sessions with a psychiatrist, but where was the follow-up after her multiple trips to the hospital? When she was released, she was dropped back into the same situation: three children and a husband, and the entire cycle started all over again.

Now, all these years later, after pulling all the information together to write my mother's story, I am just sad. Sad for my mother. Sad for my siblings who could never find it in themselves to forgive our mother for the turmoil of our youth. Sad for my father, who was robbed of the beautiful, fun-loving woman he married. Sad for my Papa and Nana, most especially my Nana, as she buried her only daughter. Sadder still that my sister followed in our mother's footsteps and led a troubled life that ended with her being classified as a 'missing person.' Sad for me, as I never got to know my mother as an adult.

All I have now are fleeting memories, like a puff of smoke. A vivacious woman with a beehive hairdo, bright red lipstick, polyester pantsuit and always smelling of Channel Number 5. Then poof, it's gone. I want to conjure it back to take a better look, but no, it's gone... for now.

Writing my mother's story gave me time to reflect and remember all the good in our world and reinforce the need for mental illness awareness and forgiveness. I long ago forgave my mother for any wrong doings she may have done, for that was not truly her. My mother was ill. Was she bipolar? I think so, or maybe it was something else, but at the end of the day, she needed help and she never really got it. I'd like to think in today's world, things would be a little different. I hope so for all the Marlenes out there.

My mother was a thoughtful, loving, and outgoing person who deserved so much better in her life. Had her illness been identified and treated, I'm certain both my parents would have had the wonderful life they had envisioned, including a blissful retirement on Salt Spring Island.

I know our mother loved us all and would have wished us the very best in our lives, and that's what I want to hold on to. Good memories, positive thoughts. As I move on through life, I always try to remember that the sun is always shining somewhere, but sometimes the clouds get in the way.

4 | Susan Henderson Frank's Story of Janet

Janet Simpson Hancock was born at home in Buckhaven, Scotland, on February 9, 1928, to Annie Whittaker Hancock, a homemaker, and James Hancock, a coal miner. Janet had an older sister named Bets.

They lived in miner's row in what was known as a 'but and ben' style of house: a two-room, one-storey, simple home with a shared outhouse toilet and no running water. A coal-burning fireplace in the main room was the only source of heat. They had a weekly bath in a big metal tub that was pulled in front of the fire and filled with hot water.

They were poor, but always very clean. For Christmas, they were lucky to get an orange. Janet was given a hand-me-down doll that was repaired by the local firemen, and she cherished her only toy. Then she was encouraged to give the doll to her cousin, who had fallen ill. Reluctantly, she gave away her cherished dolly, only to discover it discarded, broken and smashed up in the bin.

There was a family secret that Annie had given birth to two girls before she married James. She hadn't told her husband about Alice or Margaret until some years after they had been married. This news was not well-received, and Janet knew very little about her half-sisters, never connected with them, and always wondered about their lives. The only thing she knew was Alice lived on a farm and married the farmer's son.

When she was four years old, life as Janet knew it would tragically change. On March 2, 1933, Annie Hancock died at home from breast cancer. She was 42 years old.

Janet always felt sad, having lost her mom as a four-year-old child. She would forever fear that her life would end from breast cancer too. She felt so different from other little girls because she didn't have a mom. Her Dad was left to raise the two girls, and somehow, they all trudged along. Food was sparse; Janet would often go down to the seashore and pull red, spiral-shelled snails, known as buckies, from the rocks to use for soup.

When World War II broke out in 1939, every home blacked out their windows. The shrill sound of the air raid sirens would call them out to take refuge in the shelters. Everyone was issued ration books and coupons to get clothing and food. The Hancock family's meagre existence was squeezed even tighter.

As a young woman, Janet often walked the two hours to Kirkcaldy—a much larger town—to the dance hall. It was there in 1948 that she met a handsome, dark-haired, blue-eyed lad named Lawrence Henderson. Janet and Lawre courted for four years and were married on her 24th birthday in 1952.

They lived with Lawre's mom in Kirkcaldy. Janet worked as a shop assistant in Woolworth's, and Lawre worked as a mechanic. They saved their money for their dream to emigrate to Canada in the hopes of building a better life for themselves and their future children.

Lawre left for Canada first. He wanted to find a home and job before sending for Janet to join him. He worked his way across Canada and finally settled in Vancouver, a city he fell in love with, offering lots of opportunities for a mechanic.

Seven months later, in September 1953, Janet set sail on the *SS United States of America* for Canada. Once the ship landed, she took a train across Canada. The entire journey took two weeks—a brave adventure for a young woman to travel alone when she had never been further than a few miles from her home.

In her new hometown, Janet and Lawre lived in an attic apartment. They had a two-burner hot plate for cooking, and shared a down-the-hall bathroom, which she hated. Her prized possession was a second-hand Singer sewing machine set in a wooden desk with a matching stool. She loved to "make copper wire out of a penny" by shopping at yard sales, the church white elephant sales, and she stretched every dollar she earned. She worked at the Royal Bank as a teller, where many people commented that they had a hard time understanding her deep Scottish brogue.

In July of 1955, when Disneyland opened its gates, Janet, Lawre, and two of their friends packed up a car and headed south to sunny California, camping in tents along the way. Camping, however, was not a reason to let standards slip, and Janet's full-skirted, cotton dresses and matching heels were worn even to pitch a tent. A love of camping was born then that would last her lifetime. She loved the fun and frivolity of being at The Happiest Place on Earth.

By 1957, the couple had saved enough money to buy a house: a two-storey home with a large front and back yard, and, having her very own bathroom for the first time, Janet felt like she was in a palace.

In May 1957, a baby boy arrived, Bryan Charles, followed by a little girl in January 1960, Susan Laurie, both born at Grace Hospital in Vancouver.

Janet loved being a mom. All the neighbourhood children were drawn to her home. As the kids played in the yard on the swing set or with bikes, dolls, or various other toys, she would appear at the top of the stairs in her lacey apron with a tray full of Kool-Aid and cookies for all.

One of Janet's special talents was organizing and giving her children birthday parties. The table would be set with a colourful tablecloth, and bright metallic pointed hats were ready for the heads of all the tiny guests. Hot dogs and potato chips aplenty were served with a healthy dose of pop. Then the birthday cake would materialize, set ablaze with fancy candles. After the feast, the kiddies moved to games events, with a rousing competition of musical chairs, followed by 'drop the clothes pegs' in the milk bottles. After growing up with so little, Janet gave Bryan and Susan so much of what she never had.

Janet was proud to become a Canadian citizen and was also proud of her Scottish roots. She made sure her children were raised as Scots with all the opportunities that Canada offered.

The entire family returned to Scotland in 1966 for a summer

filled with family visits and trips to castles. Lawre bought a car for use during the holiday, and they toured around, having a wonderful time introducing the bairns to their family and culture in the old country.

Janet knew how to stand up for herself and use her voice to make change. She would often buy chicken breasts and was annoyed that there was skin and fat tucked under the meat because it was charged by the pound.

One time, Janet decided to save all the excess fat and skin and return it to the store. She asked to speak to the meat manager, handed him the package of surplus, and asked him to weigh it. She then asked for the price of chicken breasts and what the surplus weighed. Out came a pencil and small notebook from her elegant handbag on which she figured out the price, stuck out her hand, and said, "By my calculations, you owe me seventy-six cents."

He glared back at her, so she continued, "Do not treat us as fools. I'm here once a week and will continue to demand you pay me back for over-charging." She looked down at five-year-old Susan and said with a wink, "You have a voice, Lassie, and never ever be afraid to use it."

Janet also used her voice to petition the local government to pave the back alleys, bring in street lights, and have a mailbox installed on the corner of the street and, by golly, she got it all done!

In 1967, Janet made a decision to become a Brownie leader. Every Wednesday evening, she transformed into Brown Owl of the 116th Brownie Pack. She adored the groups of Pixies, Kelpies, Sprites, and Fairies and loved her crisp navy-blue uniform with matching felt hat. Her hair was worn in a towering brunette beehive held in place by industrial strength hair spray. Some of the girls feared that bees actually lived there.

Brown Owl-ing would occupy a good deal of Janet's time for the next five years. During her time as a Brownie leader, she would take the Brownies for one week camping trips to Camp Olave on BC's Sunshine Coast. It was a week of skill-building and fun, with the days ending sitting around a roaring campfire. Janet was gifted with a beautiful singing voice and would lead the girls in sing-alongs. Her favourite song was "Going on a Lion Hunt".

When Janet's Brownies graduated, she made each one a framed display of the badges and stripes they had earned. It was never known how many girls beyond her own daughter benefitted from Janet's generosity.

Aside from the trips to Camp Olave, Janet loved spending long, lazy summers at Cultus Lake. As soon as Bryan and Susan were out of school, Janet and Lawre would pack up the car, the trailer, the kids, and the pets and off they would go for a summer of fun in the trailer, spending their days on the lake.

In 1972, a family road trip with the trailer included a visit to Disneyland, California. Janet loved the It's a Small World ride. It was during this trip that she found a lump in her left breast. Her fear of dying like her mom was ever-present. The lump was removed, and Janet was told it was benign. However, one might wonder if she perhaps made new decisions after discovering the lump, believing her life could be shortened too.

For instance, Janet finally got her driver's license at the age of 46. It was quite the escapade going for a drive with her because she utterly refused to turn left. A ten-minute ride would turn into a detour lasting forever, with Janet trying to get to the final destination, all the while only turning right. Many trips ended in just getting lost. The maps would come out, but this was small comfort as there was no way of knowing how many dreaded left-hand turns it would entail to get back.

1975 was a summer spent travelling throughout Scotland with Lawre and Susan. Another lump had been found, and she wanted to go to Scotland to be with family before she agreed to any surgery or treatment.

In October of 1975, Janet had a mastectomy of her left breast to remove the cancer. The chemo, cobalt, and radiation treatments robbed her of her hair, vitality, and beauty and her ability to be the kind of hands-on mom she so enjoyed.

Janet survived the difficult treatments, but something in her changed. The once robust, stylish woman was now more subdued and seemed to pull back from the hustle and bustle that was once her life.

By 1977, the cancer returned. The heavy course of treatments left her weak and crying in bed on many occasions. She did her best to keep up appearances and maintain a happy home, but there was no denying she was very ill. Wigs replaced her once admired beehive.

By October 1979, knowing that she had only weeks to live—and against doctor's orders—Janet made one final trip to Scotland to say goodbye to family and friends. She stayed in Scotland for three weeks and returned home to Vancouver, where she died on October 28, 1979. Susan was only 19 when she lost her mom.

Janet was a mother, wife, Brown Owl, and a leader in her community. She was a stylish, generous, funny, creative woman who could stand up to anyone with confidence. Janet was missed and mourned by many.

SUSAN AND JANET, 1970, VANCOUVER, BC

Author Reflection - Susan Henderson Frank
Tsawwassen, BC, Canada

I was very apprehensive to write my mother's story. There was no way I wanted to relive any painful memories. Once I started writing, it was as if a flock of birds were trying to get out of my mouth. I discovered I had so much to say about her, and it all just poured out of me.

Writing my mother's story has been better than some of the therapy I have received. My broken heart, fragmented mind, and self-esteem suffered deeply from experiencing my mother's early passing. Starting in adolescence, I went down a self-destructive path. I had no way of processing the million, trillion painful things I'd witnessed. I had no one to talk to but Johnny Walker. My first blackout drunk was at age 12. I now live my life in recovery from alcoholism, but it was a long road and took a lot of work and therapy. As I write this reflection, I am 19 years sober.

My Mother's Story has given me access to the ability to connect with my mom as a whole person who lived a good and interesting life. I no longer *only* see my mom taken from me as a teenager and slowly dying from the ravages of breast cancer. This process has given me a great sense of freedom and joy to witness her life in its entirety.

As a girl, my mom taught me that I always have a right to be heard, and it's so empowering to have a venue to give a voice back to her life because no one ever talked about her after she died. It was as if she had never existed.

I knew that writing the story wasn't going to be my biggest challenge. My biggest challenge was going to be technology, or lack thereof. I had decided long ago that I would live my life without a cell phone or a computer. This work became so important to me that it forced me to rethink that decision. I was determined to give my mom's life a voice, and so I bought my first laptop. It's been challenging to overcome my lack of computer skills, but this story wanted to live, and I have persevered. In a silent tribute to my mom, my very first laptop is sleek and rose gold, as classy and elegant as her beautiful handbags.

Writing my mother's story has also allowed me to reflect on my life, and I realize that I too have lived an interesting and courageous life, and I feel really good about that.

The Story of Janet has opened up so many happy memories and helped me to fill in some of the answers to a seemingly endless list of questions.

I am so grateful for this experience and the positive changes in me. I think of my mom now with love, amazement, and laughter, instead of being caught in the past in the snare of sorrow and grief. Writing my mother's story was a spiritual gift for me.

5 | Colleen Winton's Story of Doris

When put together, the threads I have of my mother's life resemble a kind of open woven fabric, a shawl perhaps—a few bright strands with lots of holes. Still, it's comfortable enough to wrap myself in and even find some warmth.

Doris Mary Kerr (really Doris Mary *Oliveen* Kerr, though she never used her third name for reasons that should be obvious) was born November 6, 1917, in New Westminster, BC. Her mother, Emma Smither, was descended from hardy United Empire Loyalist pioneers who had travelled north to Nova Scotia and then west to New Westminster in the 1870s. Her father, William Kerr, a recent arrival, hailed from Rogersville, Indiana. Little Doris, her parents, and older brothers Billy, Russell, and Greville, lived in a large family home on the north bank of the Fraser River.

There must have always been music in the house. The boys had a bit of a band, and Doris, a slender, almost skinny youth with curly, strawberry-blonde hair, played piano and later sang with the Schubert Singers. Her father, William, an impulsive character, arrived home one day with a player piano, which was much better received than the 10-pound wheel of Limburger cheese he'd presented on another occasion and which his wife buried in the garden.

In her teens, Doris contracted rheumatic fever and was confined to bed. For months, she passed the time drawing, painting with watercolours, and listening to Nelson Eddy, one of her heartthrobs. The rheumatic fever, and resultant weakened heart, made Emma, a professional worrier, vigilant about Doris' health. A few years later, when Doris dreamed of going to a teacher's college, her mother wouldn't hear of her leaving home.

Still, Doris was a working woman all her adult life, had a number of secretarial jobs, and enjoyed a long career as a well-respected court reporter. One intriguing job along the way was Police Matron with the New Westminster Police Department. She had been the station's fingerprinter, but the Police Chief, recognizing the need for a woman in the room when handling female prisoners, had Doris sworn in.

Before she married, Doris' one big romance was with Victor, a Dutch merchant sailor. Her 5-year diary (1938-1942) is full of ecstasies over letters and telegrams received, excitement whenever he was in port, and fears of the war with Germany and the fate of his ship. The bundle of love letters from him includes one, written in Dutch (with the pencilled English translation in Doris' neat hand), from his wife in Holland. In the letter, she demands information about their relationship. (I found this deliciously scandalous, though the diary reveals Doris knew all about Victor's estranged wife. Only later did I piece together that this was the same genial Victor our family would visit in California where he lived with his new wife.)

Here's one of those holes I mentioned: I believe my parents met at a dance in 1939 where her brothers' band was playing. I don't know for certain. What I do know is that Elmer Winton, from Portage La Prairie, Manitoba (who preferred his grade nine nickname of "Pres") doted on Doris. And Pres was persistent, pursuing her throughout Doris' long-distance romance with her dashing sailor. They were engaged on Doris' 24th birthday, two years after they met, and that summer Doris married her "L'il Bug" in the back garden of the Kerr home in a simple romantic affair. More romantic, I expect, than their honeymoon on Salt Spring Island… escorted by her ever-vigilant mother.

I grew up believing my mother was a sophisticated woman who'd seen the world, but, in reality, other than an occasional trip, she never left New Westminster. In fact, she lived her whole life on one block. Mr. and Mrs. Winton spent the first five years of married life living in the Kerr house with then-widowed Emma. With 1947 came their firstborn, my sister, Sheila, who was brought home from the hospital in style in the Police Chief's car. Soon, Pres began to build Doris their own home—across the street. And then he built a small house beside that—for her mother. Doris lived the rest of her life in the house that Pres built. My brother, Peter, was born in the new house in 1950, and I arrived five years after that.

Mum loved to garden, and we always had an enormous vegetable garden, many flowerbeds and numerous fruit trees. Summer meant picking and freezing, cutting and canning, and fresh raspberries plopped directly onto your morning bowl of Shreddies. The thing her garden lacked was lilacs. On spring evenings, I would accompany my mother on her 'lilac walks' through the neighbourhood. We would stroll out with a pair of garden shears, Mum approaching each fragrant bush en route, discretely snipping a purple bloom or two from spots where they would not be missed and entrusting me with their care until we had enough to fill a vase at home.

Mum was an avid walker. Summer outings to White Rock beach often included a stroll to the Peace Arch, three kilometres away and back! Walking provided a bit of stress relief for my mother when she needed a break from my father and grandmother's favourite sport— arguing. Although Pres and Emma seemed to thoroughly enjoy their bickering, it made Mum's blood pressure rise. She hated arguing, preferring the silent treatment. Her silences could be deafening.

Mum certainly had enough stress from her job as a court reporter without more at home. In those days, the court stenographer would take down every word spoken in the courtroom on little encoding machines with their long rolls of paper, transcribing them into documents to be delivered to dozens of court officials, often on the same day. Mum would work long hours and was considered top of her field. For many years, her notes were used to train new court reporters. I was aware at some point that my mother's salary as a court reporter was actually more than my father's as a CBC Radio technician, unusual for the time, and a fact my grandmother was happy to remind my father of during their many squabbles.

My father adored my mother, and there was nothing he wouldn't do for her. Sometimes, as we sat down to dinner, he would drive

Mum crazy by abandoning the table to immediately accomplish a task she had casually mentioned needed doing. He also delighted in giving her the most exquisite custom-made jewellery. I have the sense though that, despite how full her life seemed to us, there was a restless piece of my mother that wished that some of her choices in life had been different, that Dad shared more of her interests, that life could have been more… well, *more*.

One of Mum's great loves was the Arts. She regularly attended Vancouver Symphony Orchestra concerts and on Saturdays would listen to the Met Opera broadcast in the kitchen as she caught up on ironing. When the soprano or tenor hit a high note, she would halt all conversation and activity and stand, arms outstretched, eyes closed, not breathing, drinking in the sound—until the note ended and life could resume. The smell of ironing always transports me back to those Saturdays, watching the ecstasy on her face as she listened to those notes.

She also introduced me to the singing of Ivan Rebroff, the humour of Flanders and Swann, and, when I started ballet class, shared with me her love of dance. We went to see the Bolshoi when I was about 10, and exciting as it was, what I recall most is returning home and Mum deciding we needed a late-night snack. She made us toasted bacon-and-mushroom sandwiches, which seemed to me was the most delicious, grown-up thing I had ever eaten.

As a cook, she became health conscious, and as a result, a bit adventurous. She used a wok before most people knew what one was. I loved her Steamboat, a communal and interactive fondue-like dish where an array of foods cooked on skewers in a bubbling broth, finishing with noodles simmered in the flavour-infused liquid. But I never learned to like Tiger's Milk, a hearty shake made with wheat germ and brewer's yeast. She once packed my brother off to the doctor, fearing jaundice, only to receive the diagnosis of too much carrot juice in his diet. She would throw great buffet dinner parties, made a fabulous raspberry pie using fresh berries from our garden, and I have yet to taste a pumpkin pie to rivals hers.

Mum was a crusader who fought for social and environmental

causes, started petitions, marched, and boycotted products and companies. Grapes were banned in our house to protest the treatment of migrant workers in California. Remember when you could buy bath tissue to match any colour scheme? Mum joined the fight to protect our water and successfully campaigned against the use of dyes in tissue and toilet paper.

In the mid-60s, my parents bought a piece of land and built a small cabin on Salt Spring Island, where they had honeymooned decades earlier. This became Mum's sanctuary. She was happiest when beachcombing, rowing in our bay, reading, or discovering a new skinny-dipping spot on a nearby island.

Mum had an abiding appreciation for all things classic and worthwhile. One evening, she arrived home to find me watching television well past bedtime. "What on earth are you doing up?!" she demanded. "What are you watching?" Then, glancing at the television, she melted with, "Oh, this is a marvellous play," and settled beside me to watch the rest of the classic American drama *A Raisin in the Sun*. I know she took great pleasure from my years of dancing and, though she never saw me act on stage or heard me sing, I'm certain she would have been a keen and critical supporter of my theatre career.

I remember that Mum used to sing when she sneezed—a musical coda to bring the explosion to a peaceful conclusion—Ah... ah...ACHOOOO...hmm...hm...ahum...ahum...ha...la...la... la...lalala...haaah.

I remember that, at 5'2", she was a stylish yet down-to-earth woman who wore Italian knit suits to work and slacks at home.

I remember one of her favourite sayings was, "Don't look at me in that tone of voice!" (Dorothy Parker—always steal from the best).

I do not remember the exact date my mother died. I used to know, but somehow over time, I have forgotten, and I now realize that I don't need, or want, to have a date on which to pin the remembrance. It was after her 54th birthday, I was 16, and arrived home from school to find that she had been sent home early from court with flu symptoms. From my room upstairs, I heard my father call out for me. Mum had collapsed in the bathroom. We got her into bed, but our efforts to revive her were unsuccessful. It wasn't understood then that women experience heart attacks differently from men. She deserved better.

I know that the date falls in January, between Christmas and my sister's birthday in February. The previous summer, the family had attended a Pleasure Faire, a very seven-grain, dancing-in-a-sun-drenched-field event—pure '70s—where my sister had coveted a set of pottery dishes. My mother secretly purchased them, smuggled them home, and hid them away in a linen closet to give her for Christmas. Except that she forgot about them and, upon rediscovering them after the holidays, said conspiratorially to me, "Oh well, I'll keep them for her birthday," and tucked them back under the sheets and towels.

In February, when my sister's birthday came around, Mum was gone. I went to the linen closet and uncovered the dishes, gift wrapped them, and gave them to my sister. She received them with delight and confusion. Here they were, strange and familiar, miraculous; a present only Mum could have purchased. It was as though I had given her a piece of Mum back.

DORIS, CIRCA 1940

Author Reflection - Colleen Winton
New Westminster, BC, Canada

I wrote my Story of Doris in 2005, as part of the 'original' group of women who hosted gatherings in our homes to witness each other's writing, chronicling our ordinary mothers and their extraordinary lives. I initially didn't feel as though I belonged with these women, most of whose mothers were still very much alive.

How I envied their privilege in having adult relationships with their mothers. There was so much about mine I didn't know. What could I write? How could I do her justice? I had a faulty memory and flimsy artefacts. Her 5-year diary that had been disappointing to me as a teenager—so much description of the weather—I now approached with the forensic curiosity of an archaeologist. I pieced together as much as I could. I let my older sister read my first draft, and she responded with tears and tales, facts I had misremembered and fascinating details I simply didn't know.

It was empowering to put Doris' story into words. A woman whose life had somehow seemed 'less than' because it was briefer than others was now given its due. Some in the group were curious as to how, precisely, my mother had died. But that to me seemed beside the point. I wanted to write about her life, not her death. Her death was about my loss. I hadn't embarked on this as a healing journey. It was not about me.

In this new collection of writers, I again felt somewhat outside the process. I envied the kinship of the therapeutic group to which some belonged. They were healing through writing, with exercises to propel their work. Doris' story, captured 17 years ago, hadn't changed. Should I rewrite it? If I were to write it now, would I approach it differently? Would it then be about my new perspective, my loss, and not about her? I connected with one of the exercises—What did your mother teach you? I made a list.

Doris taught me to:
- stand up for what you believe
- stand up for the Earth
- fight against the things you believe are wrong
- have your own money
- wear sensible shoes
- appreciate the Arts
- plant a garden
- eat healthily
- go for a walk

As someone in the group remarked, it's a good list.

In the end, with some minor tweaks, Doris' story remains in its original form. Recognizing what she taught me is enough. Reflecting on her story now, having lived beyond the age at which my mother died—a significant milestone—I feel for my mother's loss, not my own. What would her favourite activities with her grandsons be? Which writers would she admire? Would she prefer the singing of Bryn Terfel or Ben Heppner? What causes would she be fighting for? There's so much I wish she could have known, so much I want to teach her.

If I could rewrite her life, I would make it longer.

6 | Jin Beom Synn's Story of Myeong-rae Park

I have only limited information about my mother, Myeong-rae Park, because she passed away when I was in second grade and just nine years old. I have two photos of my mother, both taken on the day of an elementary school picnic. She wore traditional Korean clothes called *hanbok*. In the faded pictures, my mother was seated, her hair pulled back neatly in a bun and secured with a large hairpin, and she held a paper fan. Her posture was gracious, but her expression does not seem happy or peaceful. Truth was, she attended that day solely for her youngest child, even though she may have been in a terrible condition. It was my only and last picnic with my mother.

Myeong-rae Park was born on May 11, 1931. She was the eldest daughter with one sister and two brothers. I do not know the names or ages of her siblings, nor her parent's names. They lived in a deep rural area where buses only ran four times per day. They grew mushrooms and rice and were very poor. In my mother's childhood, she could not receive a decent education, or even food and meals. Food was scarce, which made her very weak.

My mother's youngest brother had a disabled arm, ending at the wrist, with no hand. She probably felt very sorry for her brother's condition and worked even harder to make up for this. Even though she was not a physically strong woman, she devoted herself to her family as a first child, like the giving tree in Shel Silverstein's work.

My mother married my father, named Gi-seong Synn, at the age of 17 in 1950. My mother's family religion was Catholicism. However, because my father's family was Buddhist, by tradition, my mother had to convert her religion. That was a frequent custom at that time. Ironically, among her children, all except my brother became Catholics. But either way, we all remember our mother in our prayers.

My father was the second son of 11 sisters and brothers, and the first son of the family had gone abroad when he was young. So, my father had to play the role of the eldest son, which meant my mom had to help take care of a large family.

During the Korean War, my father's military service was much longer than the peace time soldiers, thus making my mother solely responsible for the support of my father's siblings. My father was eleven years older than my mother, which meant there seemed to a big generation gap between them. Thus, they didn't share common themes and hobbies or have long conversations.

Mom had eight children—four boys (Mu-beom, Seok-beom, me, and another brother whose name I don't know), and four girls (Oak-hee, Chu-hee, Yeon-hee, Mee-hee). We are all two or three years apart, and I am her youngest son.

Her eldest son was lost to a tragic death, passing right before entering elementary school because of a sudden illness of some sort. At that time, my father, celebrating his first son's education, bought a fancy school bag for him, which became a sad artefact reminding of his sudden absence. Since their eldest son's death, my parents led sad and heartbroken lives.

When their third son also passed away at an early age (the cause of which I do not know), my parents thought they needed one more boy to strengthen our clan. At that time, people placed more value on sons under the patriarchal and Confucian traditions. Sons were supposed to succeed to their family trees and lead the ritual for dead ancestors, so most parents thought that having only one son was not 'safe enough.' So, they had two more daughters and then me.

My mother's cooking skills were excellent; so much so that I have heard villagers frequently visited our house to enjoy the invigorating menu of my mother when they lost their appetite for their own meals.

Mom used to tell me she wanted to weed the flower bed of heaven. I couldn't understand why because she already had to endure her endless toils at the orchards, rice paddies, and our house. I heard that she would sometimes neglect her meals to weed more grass. I imagine she would be wonderful at caring for a heavenly garden.

I really liked the small, round buns my mom made with simple ingredients of flour and sugar. She knew how much I loved those buns, and no matter how ill and tired she was, she would give in to my invincible, childish tantrums. When I was young, I was a very picky eater. My mom always chased me around the small table to make me eat more than a spoonful of rice. We were, in a sense, like the Disney characters, Tom and Jerry.

Mom is linked to an unforgettable, sad, happy—and a little perplexing—episode about making me take cold medicine. When I was young, I was a frequent patient having various illnesses. Mom used to make me take bitter, powdered medicine by carefully mixing it with water on a spoon using her pinky finger. Remembering the medicine's bitter taste, I would try to run away through the room where we had our supper. My family stopped my narrow escape, thwarted by an older sister and my parents. They seized me strongly and held me still, so I had to take the medicine.

At that moment, an idea occurred to me. I collapsed like a dead possum before my family. My awkward acting was so real, my sister cried and shouted, "Jin Beom was killed by our parents forcing him to take medicine!" My mom was so shocked that she threw the spoon and was about to wail aloud. I, who became so suffocated, moved again, feeling shame and guilt. That night, my mom again prepared the bitter medicine, and I took it. My family frequently talks about this funny episode when thinking about our mom.

Some people have told me that my father was not an easy-going person, who frequently enjoyed alcohol and sometimes engaged in unsettling behaviour, like breaking a gate or being unkind while feeding animals in the house. Hence, my mother suffered due to various problems my father had endlessly caused. She worked very hard as a farmer's wife and couldn't know the proper ways to express her fear, anger, worries, and anxiety because she always took the burden of her lonely life like a sponge.

Among the hardships and toils, my mother sometimes had happy moments. One of them is the moment that she heard me sing through my elementary school loudspeaker. At that time, she and my father were picking apples at the big orchard. They heard my song spreading from the faraway school and took a short break and applauded heartily. I later came to know that they really enjoyed my song, which was actually the performance of a novice who sang and hummed frequently.

My mother's accumulated hardships caused a lot of stress and frequently made her ill. At that time, she could not make the long journey to go to a clinic or the hospital due to obligations such as house chores and field or orchard work. It was common for residents of rural populations to endure discomfort for long periods of time. Even though she had bad symptoms of a weak and ailing stomach, Mom could only try to alleviate her symptoms by drinking soda water or perhaps with some liquid medicine sold at a rural drugstore. All that time, when she did not seek medical attention, it was not 'just' a weak stomach, but stomach cancer that was brewing. By the time my mother was able to go to the hospital, her stomach was swollen, and the cancer had progressed.

After her cancer operation, my mother's condition became worse. She couldn't move from bed and was always laying weakly. Her lips were dry, so we gave her water and sweet juice and the inner parts of grapes with a spoon. I remember seeing her balloon-like belly. At that time, we, like other people living in rural areas, applied Korean folk remedies to cure my mother's cancer. Sometimes, steamed yellow pumpkins were laid on my mother's swollen stomach.

My father, who felt remorse and sympathy and regretted his misbehaviour, resorted to Korean shamans, *Mudangs*, who tried to exorcise the bad ghost-like illness by chanting ritual songs and prayers, playing drums, gongs, and cymbals in the middle of night, and as the strongest weapon, throwing scary kitchen knives to scare the devil called stomach cancer. All methods turned-out to be useless.

My mother passed away at the age of 45, in 1976, after she had a second attack of her disease. I could only live with her for nine years.

I am sorry for her short life in this world.

I imagine my mother reciting a poem, which I envision she may have written while happily weeding the flower beds of heaven…

My beloved son,

I am happy to see what and who you are.
I have seen all your endless efforts
I have heard all your prayers and sighs
I have known your loneliness for a long time

Do you know?
I have also prayed for your wellbeing and happiness

I am happy to have my voice in your writing
You depicted my inner feeling and sufferings which I could not express
for several reasons

Your writing is a powerful condolence to me.
In this heavenly garden, I find many mothers who passed away at
their early age.

We always sing and pray for our children.
So, our children, take heart and live your precious lives with all your
souls until we meet here.

Read many good poems and literary works.
Seek to make the world better and livable place and protect this earth.

Due to your memorial, your writing
I feel that my cup is full, and I am very proud of you.

I am very happy
Until we meet in this paradise
Let me make this flower garden more beautiful

MYEONG-RAE, 1975, GYEONGSANGBUK PROVINCE, KOREA

Author Reflection - Jin Beom Synn

Seoul, South Korea

I came to know death at a very early age. Whenever I thought of Mom's passing, I felt intense agony related to death. Sometimes, I couldn't breathe evenly and sprang out from the sleeping mattress.

When someone in our village died, villagers decorated wooden funeral biers, which are like modern-day hearses, with colourful paper flowers that the pallbearers carried, singing sad songs at the top of their voices, and swinging a small bell. After my mom's funeral, I had made it a rule to run away and avoid seeing hearses and biers. That was my biggest trauma.

Now, at the age of fifty-four, I have overcome the invincible fear of death. When I see a hearse, I pray for the deceased person's soul. Here in South Korea, people say that when we see a hearse passing, we have a lucky day; ancient wisdom making death both a natural flow and a step to other spiritual worlds.

My mom does not have a tomb to visit because she was cremated, and her powdered bones were scattered in the air. So, in fact, she is anywhere and everywhere. Now, I can meet my beloved mom whenever I like, just looking up to the heaven to embrace and hug her.

People thought highly of my mom; they praised her kind heart and enduring attitudes, saying that she was an angel in the form of a human. I have sought to resemble her wonderful traits. And like her—merciful, gracious, and lovely solitary reaper and gardener in heaven—I keep a small garden on the veranda of my apartment, always thinking of her heavenly garden filled with beautiful and colourful flowers.

Writing my mother's story was very challenging for me; even more than I could have imagined. For several months, I devoted myself to this wonderful project. I knew so little about my mother; I had to gather her lost information to give her a voice. I wanted to give my mom that voice through 'her' poem and envisioned her in a heavenly flower bed while composing—its healing power welling-up inside me and permitting me to finally send the message to my mom in heaven. I imagine she continues to send bright and generous smiles and prayers, as if she knows all my loneliness, hardships, sorrows, longings, happiness, and successes.

These efforts included our wonderful, sad, and moving workshop sessions with other anthology authors, which were an unforgettable part of the healing process. I believe that I was only able to send my delayed 'unsent letter' to my mom in heaven after giving her a more proper mourning. My humble wish is that those who will read our mothers' stories and our experiences of writing about our mothers can find hope, brightness, and surviving strategies following our traces.

Now, I am not a doctor who can cure the physical or mental illness of people. However, I am a professor conducting research on bibliotherapy and American novels and can help let heartbroken people express their trauma for their wellbeing. I seek to help people suffering from heartbreak find the secret of life and survive whole. I think what I am doing is closely related with my mother's short life.

Writing my mother's story helped me remember that Mom will always pray for me, and I will always look up to her, thank her for her endless care and love, and for making my own family love and cherish each other and remember my mom's heritage and life.

7 | Kathryn Lannan's Story of Karen

Karen Grace Coates was born on July 29, 1956, in Botwood, Newfoundland. She was the sixth daughter born to Merle and Rose Coates, their eighth child of ten. Like most of her siblings, she was a summer baby. Her father worked down on the wharf as a longshoreman for the local paper company and, although he made good money, work was often not steady because of the weather. Her mother stayed at home and always bragged that she could peel ten pounds of potatoes on a Kleenex as she made dinner. Back then, Commonwealth Drive was a place filled with childhood noise while Mother listened doing the dishes and Father gardened or played cribbage at the dining room table.

As a child, Karen loved singing opera at the top of her lungs, and as a teenager was obsessed with local hockey, cheerleading, and watching roller derby on TV. She would take her two youngest sisters, Rosemary and Dawn, down to the airbase to get some fries. At sixteen, she sat on the middle stair to the upper floor staring out the window in the hopes of seeing Earl Jennings drive by in his old car, listening to Bob Dylan. Her teenage crush was forbidden because he was ten years older than her—he had just graduated university and Karen was in junior high. Their worlds were so different that Karen began to dream of life off The Rock.

Karen left The Rock after graduating from high school and moved to Ottawa to be with her older sister Sonia—a bold move for a bold girl. Her days of going down to the airbase to get some fries with her two youngest sisters were gone, leaving them in a much quieter home. A home that once saw at least eight of the ten kids grow became nearly an empty nest. All her older siblings had grown and left the house. Even though the house was now quieter, it was still the epicentre of the Coates' family; the family's beacon.

Karen and her sister Sonia rented a basement suite with another girl, and Karen got a job at Canadian Tire. She would come home after work looking forward to her can of Coke waiting in the fridge, but it would always be gone—the roommate was always taking her things! In the summer of 1974, her brother Munden married Linda in Ottawa and Karen was included in the bridal party. Munden was the younger of her two brothers and seven years older than her. Harold was her oldest brother.

Karen was a beautiful young woman with a smile you couldn't forget. When she wasn't working, she would go to dances and pubs where she met many of her brother's Italian coworkers; the most memorable of whom was a man named Sabastian. He was one of many men who would have given anything to be her boyfriend. But Karen was a free spirit, a liberated woman who knew in her heart who she really wanted.

After a year in Ottawa, Karen moved back to Botwood and took a job at the Woolco in Grand Falls. To her mother's dismay, Karen had no qualms driving 45 minutes to work, even in the snow. She was a hard worker and had an amazing work ethic. In the workplace, she was loved for her attitude and humour. She wanted a car and beautiful clothes but always insisted on earning her own things. One of her most prized purchases was her white go-go boots.

She loved to spoil her younger sisters with special gifts like Super Slider skates. She saved up for her first car, a powder blue Ford Maverick. But at one point, she could not afford her car insurance. Her older sister Gwen, visiting from British Columbia, watched a devastated Karen cry and cry on the middle stair looking out at her car in the driveway. Neither Merle nor Rose could handle their daughter's sobs. Karen was relieved when she heard her mother say, "For God's sakes, Merle, go get her some insurance!" And he did!

Karen was happy to be home. Even though Botwood was a small town, it was the big town to the smaller communities surrounding it. Many young people would visit to have some excitement. When Karen came home, there was a buzz around town that she was back.

One day, as she walked the main drag, she met another Karen who had come from one of these smaller communities. They quickly became friends. Karen invited her to move into the family home, convincing her by saying, "Mom's always got a great dinner on." To avoid any confusion, they became Karen One and Karen Two.

Karen One was now 21, and she began to sometimes date Earl, their age difference no longer seeming so vast. But he was living off the grid in a fishing shack, and this was not ideal for Karen. So yet again, their love was paused.

Around 1978, Karen Two introduced Karen One to Robert, whom she worked in broadcasting with. They hit it off right away. Robert offered the stability that Karen wanted. A year later, Karen and Robert were married in her hometown in the Anglican church. Her seven sisters and two new sisters-in-law were her bridesmaids, dressed in beautiful yellow summer dresses. After their wedding, they moved to St. John's and a year later to Carbonear, Newfoundland.

In 1980, Karen was diagnosed with ovarian cancer; she was twenty-three years old. She thought she was pregnant because her stomach had become enlarged, but she wasn't. She was told it was a slow, non-aggressive cancer. Karen wanted to be a mom. The doctor said she would live long enough to see her children grow and most likely graduate university. Karen didn't accept that she had cancer and did not deal well with her diagnosis, and neither did her husband. They both wanted to start a family, and so she started taking mild chemotherapy pills in the hope that she could still become a mom.

In 1981, Karen discovered she was pregnant and stopped all treatments. On February 4, 1982, their first daughter, Jennifer—a beautiful baby with brown curly hair—was born. Then fourteen months later, on April 16, 1983, their second daughter, Kathryn, came into the world. All the babies in this family were treasured, doted on, and adored by Karen's siblings, who took turns flying in to kiss every little cheek.

Karen felt that as long as she could still become pregnant, her cancer diagnosis could not be true. This denial was deep rooted, and Karen declined many treatments as the cancer progressed.

However, her dream of watching her daughters graduate became less of a reality. In 1985, a spot showed up in an x-ray of her left lung. She had an invasive surgery that left a large scar, not only on her body but on her spirit. Her parents came to Carbonear to help her recover, as did many siblings during these difficult times. Karen periodically received some chemotherapy, but she never finished an entire treatment plan.

In 1985, when Robert was transferred to St John's, they bought a new home on a cul-de-sac. Karen became pregnant again but lost the baby. The cancer became more aggressive. She fell into a deep depression and was medicated with tranquillizers, spending most of her time in bed. Her two young children were left to fend for themselves, growing up with *Sesame Street* as their babysitter. With her mental and physical health declining, so was Karen's marriage. When it became obvious that her husband was having an affair, their fighting escalated, even in front of the girls.

In 1988, after their last fight as husband and wife, Karen packed up her two daughters and drove the five hours west back to Botwood to her parents' house. Back to her family home and beacon. News travelled fast, and the first person waiting for her was Earl. Now a single mom, with two young daughters and a diagnosis that was grim, she needed her family more than ever.

Once she was able to get her own apartment, Karen tried to build a life for her girls the best she could. Earl and Karen became inseparable, and he treated her daughters like they were his own. Earl wanted to marry Karen but wouldn't unless she received treatment. Karen couldn't accept that she had cancer, and although Earl loved her, he wouldn't marry her.

Much of Karen's last years were spent with family, travelling to Mount Pearl to see Rosemary, and Ontario to see Lorraine, Sonia, and Kathryn. Her sister Dawn lived in Botwood, and their eldest sister, Pauline, lived in Bishop's Falls, not far away, so many nights were spent having hen parties with the cousins playing with the Easy-Bake oven and the sisters giving each other home perms.

When it was time, Karen enrolled her daughters at Botwood

Academy, her old elementary school, and celebrated with her girls by going down to the airbase for ice cream. After Jennifer's birthday, with snow still on the ground, the girls were sent to Munden's home in La Scie for a couple of months while Karen dealt with medical appointments and tried to pull herself back together. It was long enough that they were formally enrolled in school. The girls came back to Botwood just before the end of the school year, and Karen was able to watch Kathryn graduate kindergarten and Jennifer finish grade two. This would be the only graduation she would get to celebrate.

In November 1989, Karen was told that her cancer was now terminal. She begged and pleaded with the doctors to make her better. She was now ready to take the chemo and do whatever it took. Earl and her family had pleaded with her for years to seek the treatments she was offered, but it was simply too late. Notes in her chart at the end of her hospital bed read, "keep her comfortable."

Karen's last Christmas was spent in hospital. Sonia and Bruce brought the girls to St. John's to be with her. Their last visit, on Boxing Day, was amongst hallways of endless doors opening into brown interiors and in hospital waiting rooms. Karen, as a mother, had spent a lot of time in and out of hospitals, but her love for her girls was always known. Unfortunately, the natural progression of ovarian cancer had now run its course.

On the morning of January 1, 1990, Karen passed away at the Health Sciences Centre in St. John's, with Lorraine, her husband Larry, Rosemary, and Earl by her side. She was 33 years old; Jennifer was seven, and Kathryn was six. When the news travelled by phone to Commonwealth Drive, a box of tissues was passed around. A little later that day, Munden, Sonia, and Bruce took the girls outside to build a snowman in the fresh snow. Pauline's family joined in when they arrived. After every snowstorm, Newfoundland families would bundle up and venture outside to build tunnels, forts, and snowmen; it was tradition.

Karen was the only family member to be christened, confirmed, married, and buried at St. James Anglican church in Botwood, which gave her mother solace that all these milestones of her life had been held there. Before the funeral, her daughters placed pictures they drew in the casket as they said their final goodbye. Earl placed a wedding ring on a gold chain around her neck. Twenty-nine years later, when he died, he was buried next to Karen—as was their promise to one another.

KAREN, 1976, IN A FAVOURITE DRESS

Author Reflection - Kathyrn Lannan
Nanaimo, BC, Canada

In 2018, I participated in an Ovarian Cancer Walk of Hope with my family. When I walked through the arch at the end, the sadness and grief surrounding the pain of losing my mom sparked a healing journey. When I started the *My Mother's Story* project, I didn't really know who my mom was—I was only six when she passed away. I realized that over the last 30 years, much of the grief surrounding my mom kept me as this little six-year-old girl.

As I moved to a place of acceptance, giving my mom a place in the world and a voice became a very important part of this journey. I only knew her story as my mom. I knew what she looked like from photos, but I didn't know what her favourite song was. After she passed away, she was erased from my life completely, but I craved to know who she was. So, I allowed myself to discover who she was through conversations with her siblings. I was able to create a narrative of her whole life and capture a beautiful love story between her and Earl, a story she deserved and one I never knew.

I often wonder what my life would have looked like had she not passed away. I wonder what kind of Gran she would have been. I wonder what she would look like now. I wonder who I would be if I had not had to move across Canada after her death and been cut off from all communication with her family.

After twelve years, when I was 19, my mom's family finally found me again. That moment changed my whole life. I would have never been able to become a barber if it weren't for an inheritance that had been put aside for me by my grandparents, Mommy and Daddy Coates, to be given to me when I was 20. Even though many of my formative years were spent without my mother, she and her family gave me my future.

I felt her presence with me in the hospital when I became a mom on the 16th anniversary of my mom's death. The room glowed, and I could feel her sitting in the rocking chair beside my hospital bed.

This remains one of the most profound moments in my life. I have carried this feeling every day in my heart. She gave me life, and as a result, I too experienced the gift of being a mom, the one thing she always wanted to be.

I could not have written this story without my aunts and uncles, who spent hours on the phone with me, sharing beautiful, funny, and sometimes sad stories about their sister. Children that lose their parents become orphans; people who lose a spouse become widows or widowers. But for my aunts and uncles, there is no term for losing a sibling or for their survivor's guilt. *My Mother's Story* has helped all of us to speak of her. Although Karen's story is short, she brought so many people together.

I may not have been given the easiest road. Nonetheless, I continue to travel it with strength and resiliency because that's what my mother's death has given me. To this day, I am forever grateful to her and feel her presence with me. I find dimes in places where they shouldn't be, and I know it's her. Sometimes I find them at the bottom of the laundry basket, one single dime, or I go to get into my vehicle, and there is a dime on the seat. When I find one, I have a reflective moment about my mother, and then I add it to the collection on the mantle. These dimes have now become her voice.

8 | Sydell Weiner's Story of Janet

My mother was born on May 5, 1917, in Rochester, New York. Her parents both emigrated from Eastern Europe, lured by the promise of a better life. Her father, Abraham Kay (born Kosovsky), came from Belarus in 1911, and her mother, Edith Garelick, from Poland in 1913. They were married in New York City on December 22, 1913, when Abe was 19 and Edith was 17.

My mother, Janet, was their first child and was followed three years later by Alice and by Beverly six years after that. They enjoyed a comfortable lifestyle in Rochester, a beautiful city in upstate New York, where Janet learned to appreciate both opera and horseback riding. She was a better-than-average student and made friends easily, but by the time she was fifteen, the family moved 300 miles away to Brooklyn, New York. Abe had been a successful salesman and was about to run his own business in a garment factory. Janet was pretty, poised, and popular, attracting the attention of many young men. She was also a born leader and took great satisfaction in running a girls' club for teenagers who needed a big sister.

In 1937, she met Milton Horowitz. He may not have been as well off as some of her boyfriends, but he had a great sense of humour and was smart as a whip. She was the refined, beautiful girl from Rochester falling in love with the boy from the lower east side. But Milton had just finished law school, and he showered her with attention, kept her laughing and made her feel like the most beautiful girl in the world. It was clear they were a match, and married on March 24, 1939, in New York City when Janet was 22 and Milt was 25.

The wedding was an exquisite, formal affair, with nine bridesmaids in matching silk gowns and nine groomsmen in tuxedos. Janet and Milton were the oldest in their respective families, and her parents loved him immediately. Wages were low in 1939, but Milt got a raise to $6.00 a week as a law clerk when they got married, and Janet worked as a bookkeeper. They honeymooned in Florida and returned to an apartment in the Bensonhurst neighbourhood of Brooklyn.

They lived on the same block as her sister Alice and husband Jess, and they all became best friends. This made her first year as Janet Horowitz especially fun, and on May 6, 1943, it got even better. One day after her 26th birthday, Nancy Roberta was born, and the couple became a family. The war in Europe was escalating, but Milt thought he'd be exempt from serving since he was a lawyer and had a new baby. Nevertheless, when Nancy was six months old, Milt was drafted into the Army.

Janet followed her husband to North Carolina while he was in basic training. But when he was shipped overseas in 1944, she returned to New York and worked for WAVES (Women Accepted for Volunteer Emergency Services). It was difficult raising her daughter alone, but when Milton returned in 1946, they went on a second honeymoon to Miami Beach to celebrate.

Their second daughter, Sydell Sally, was born on February 18, 1947, when Janet was 29. Alice and Jess had two sons almost the same age as Janet's daughters, so everyone shared responsibilities. It was a happy time for her, being close to family and staying home with her girls. Milt was doing well in his law practice in Manhattan, and they even snuck away on a vacation in 1951 to Toronto and Lake George, where Janet got to do some horseback riding. But it was when Milt bought her a mink coat that she knew she had arrived. In the 1950s, it was a huge status symbol, and she was proud to be the wife of a successful lawyer.

Janet was ambitious, not only for herself but for her daughters. Nancy was especially pretty, and Janet took her into Manhattan to get professional pictures so she could do some modelling. Nancy did well, and when Sydell turned five, Janet got pictures for her too. But by 1952, the family was moving to the suburbs of Long Island and going 30 miles into the city for photo shoots was just too much. The new house in Mineola was Janet's dream, and when they moved in, she couldn't have been happier.

Although they didn't see their families quite as often, they still got together many times a year for the Jewish holidays. There were always at least 20 around the table, the food was plentiful, and the atmosphere warm. Once Janet settled into suburban life, she and Milt got involved in the building of a new synagogue. She became President of the Sisterhood and began volunteering at many charitable organizations. She was a volunteer at Long Island Jewish Hospital and became President of the local chapter of The United Cerebral Palsy Association. She was great at organizing meetings and events and loved entertaining friends at her home.

On a December morning in 1954, however, Janet got a phone call that rocked her world. Her father, Abraham Kay, had been found dead in his factory. They assumed it was a heart attack, but when they found him, he was hanging from a rope, having committed suicide. He was possibly embezzling money from the business, and, seeing no other way out, had ended his life. This was traumatic for Janet, who adored her father, but she fought to maintain a façade to keep the shameful secret from everyone she knew.

There is a lot written about the relationship between mind and body when it comes to disease. Could the trauma of her father's suicide have activated a dormant genetic anomaly? Regardless of the root cause, in February of 1956, when Janet was 38 years old, she was diagnosed with breast cancer. She was a no-nonsense woman, and matter-of-factly told her daughters that she was going into the hospital to have a breast removed. Nancy was twelve, and Sydell was eight at the time, but the word "cancer" was never used, and she reassured them that everything would be fine.

Fortunately, Janet recovered well from the surgery, and life continued as if nothing had gone wrong. The family went on vacation to Washington, DC, where everyone had fun, and no mention was made of her recent mastectomy. To help other women who'd had the same surgery, Janet made a point of visiting them in the hospital.

She comforted them and willingly gave her friendship. Ruth Schwartz was one such woman. Their families became close, and Ruth became a trusted friend for many years to come.

But by 1957, Janet's hospital work came to a sudden halt. There was a lump in her other breast. The doctor told Milt that it was probably the breast cancer coming back, but to remove her other breast would be too upsetting for her. There was no chemotherapy in those days, so without including Janet, the doctor and Milt chose to treat it with radiation. I know it's astounding by today's standards, but in those days, husbands made decisions for their wives. They often decided if the wife should even be told the truth about her diagnosis. Janet was not told.

By the end of 1958, the atmosphere around the home changed as the cancer silently progressed. Janet's health and state of mind were both unpredictable. She was in and out of the hospital, one day quite ill, and the next getting dressed in her nylons and heels to attend a charity luncheon. On her bad days, she was short tempered and frequently irritated by her daughters, who were also kept from the truth. She yelled at them and seemed to blow up over the smallest infractions. On her good days, however, she would play her opera records and bustle around the house. She continued to get her long, beautiful nails manicured in her signature bright red, and she also remained ambitious for her girls.

In 1959, Janet took 12-year-old Sydell into Manhattan to enroll her in the American Academy of Dramatic Arts. Nancy had been the model, but Sydell would be the actress. Going alone on the train into the city was fun for Sydell and kept her distracted from what was going on at home. Janet was weakening, but she still had her good days. She was proud of her daughters and enjoyed planning Sydell's Bat Mitzvah in February of 1960. At 42, she remained a gracious hostess and looked beautiful at the party, although in some of the pictures, one of her eyes seems to be closing.

The cancer had reached her brain by that time, and nobody said a word. Several months later, when Janet became so sick, she had to be rushed to the hospital, the cover-up continued. It was hepatitis, she was told, and everyone went along.

By February of 1961, Janet had more bad days than good. Nonetheless, she and Milt celebrated the 5-year anniversary of her mastectomy as evidence that she was cancer free and was going to get better. But by May, she had taken a turn for the worse.

One afternoon, she got out of bed to go to the bathroom and was so weak that she fell right there on the floor. A neighbour was called in to help her up, and a nurse's aide was subsequently hired to assist her during the day. No conversation took place in the family. Milt went to work, and the girls went to school, and it was never acknowledged that she was dying of cancer.

Inevitably, on May 26, 1961, just weeks after turning 44, Janet Kay Horowitz passed away. She left two daughters, then 14 and 18, with no explanation or words of goodbye. Did she know she was dying? Did she know that the cancer had returned? Or was the need to be strong more important than the truth? Cancer was whispered about in those days, and breast cancer, in particular, was stigmatized as a curse. There were no marathons, pink ribbons or celebrities trumpeting their cause. There were only secrets and lies. And in that environment, the life of my mother was cut short.

Just as illness was kept secret in the 1950s, so was grief. After she died, her husband couldn't talk about her, so her children followed suit. The memories faded, and the subject became taboo. But her life mattered, and she deserves to be remembered.

Janet Kay Horowitz was a beauty in her youth, a leader in her community, ambitious for her children and a proud and loving wife. She was tall and slim and always confident in social situations. She loved her parents and her sisters and their children and was equally warm to her husband's extended family. She was strong and efficient, and always tried to look her best and do what was expected. She cooked dinner every night in high heels and dresses and never complained about it.

My mother would be proud of the legacy she left behind. Her husband of 22 years found love again and continued to make people laugh. Nancy married Ruth Schwartz's son and had three beautiful children, who all distinguished themselves in their careers. Nancy had four grandchildren that Janet would have loved. I became a drama professor, thanks to my mother's push, and then a marriage and family therapist. My son is a rabbi, a hospital chaplain, and a leader in his community. My daughter has the poise and confidence of her grandmother, with a successful career to boot. Between the two of them, I have seven beautiful grandchildren.

Janet Horowitz's life may have been all too short, but as her youngest daughter, I refuse to let her memory be forgotten.

JANET, JANUARY 1946

Author Reflection - Sydell Weiner
Los Angeles, California, USA

It's been over 60 years since my mother died. When I began to write my mother's story in 2016, her generation of family was long gone. She was rarely mentioned by my father or even my sister, and the memories had begun to fade.

But I had boxes of pictures that relatives had given me over the years. I pulled out all the photos and tried to arrange them chronologically. I knew my mother was born in Rochester, so I studied the backgrounds in her childhood pictures. I was able to guess what activities she liked and when her family moved to Brooklyn.

I found her wedding pictures, which gave me even more details. My father, who died in 2002 at the age of 88, had never spoken of it. Once he remarried, five years after she passed, the subject of my mother became taboo. In fact, my father's dying words to me were how Lila, his 2nd wife, was the love of his life.

When I wrote my mother's story, I sent my sister the first draft. She confirmed some of the details for accuracy, but our feelings surrounding that time in our lives had never been broached. Nancy lives in Florida, and I live in California, so our visits over the years had been sporadic. But three years ago, when she had a minor surgery, I stayed with her for a week to help her convalesce. It gave me the opportunity to bring up some long-hidden memories that I needed to share.

One morning, Nancy asked me to help her wash her hair in the sink. As I scrubbed her scalp, I had an image of my mother watching her two girls taking care of each other. "Mommy would be so happy to see us together right now," I whispered, speaking the only name we had ever used for her. Nancy warmed and began to smile, so I went on. "I always think of the morning she died. She was sleeping, and I tiptoed out of the house so I wouldn't wake her and have to get her pills. I wish I had stopped and at least said goodbye."

My sister sighed. "I must have left after you. I went into her room and asked her how she felt. 'A little better,' she answered, which is what she always said to me. And then I told her, 'Good, I love you'."

It was like the sun had finally come out from behind the shadows. "Oh, Nancy," I said, "I'm so happy she got that from one of her daughters. That must have been the last thing she heard before she died."

Rewriting my mother's story for this *Gone Too Soon* anthology made me realize that most of what I remember about her life revolved around her death. I didn't get to tell her then, but I hope that sharing her story is a way I can say "I love you" now.

Somehow, I think she already knew.

9 | Christine Norris' Story of Chrissie

Christina MacDonald Law ("Chrissie") was born in Montreal on March 20, 1915, to James Law and Janet Anderson ("Jenny"), who had emigrated separately from Scotland in 1909. Jenny had come to Montreal to join her older sister, Mary. Jenny and James met at the local Presbyterian church, which mostly had Scottish members. They were married the following year. James and Jenny's first child, Tom, was born in 1911, four years before Chrissie.

When Chrissie was five, her widowed grandmother, Christina MacDonald Anderson (after whom she had been named in the Scottish tradition), moved to Montreal to be with her daughters, Mary, and Jenny. When Chrissie was 11, another of Jenny's sisters, Lizzie, who had been recently widowed, and her six-year-old daughter, Nancy, also joined them in Montreal. So, Chrissie's early life was full of family. Her cousin, Nancy, was like a sister to her all through her life.

Chrissie went to the local English school. In her primary classes, there was a young boy named Leonard, who, many years later, would become her husband. Chrissie was eight months older than Leonard. In their Grade 3 photo, she was one of the tallest in the class and he was the shortest. By the time they were teenagers, Leonard had become an inch or so taller than Chrissie. However, she was still a tall person, just like her dad.

Sadly, Chrissie's mother, Jenny, died when Chrissie was 18. Chrissie had finished high school by then and was working as a housekeeper for a family in the upscale district of the Town of Mount Royal. Less than two years after Jenny died, James Law married a woman named Cathy from the church. Cathy was a great housekeeper and cook. She was well known in the church community because she had been a cook in a castle in Scotland.

However, Cathy, with all her positive attributes, had one negative characteristic: a sharp tongue. Chrissie, who was very sensitive to criticism, no longer felt comfortable at home and found a way to live with the family she worked for. Chrissie loved to play the piano, and the Town of Mount Royal family encouraged her to play theirs.

Around that time, Chrissie met Olive, a Scottish friend who went to her church. Olive had a boyfriend, Andrew, and his friend, Leonard, Chrissie's old Grade 3 classmate, became her boyfriend. This wasn't an amazing coincidence; they all went to the same church, which was the centre of their world. Because the English-speaking citizens were in the minority in Montreal, especially in the east end, the church became the place where they made friends and found boyfriends and girlfriends. Chrissie and Leonard were married in 1938. She had just turned 23, and he was 22.

The newlyweds went to Ottawa for their honeymoon. It was the farthest Chrissie had ever been from home. The idea of travelling and seeing new places really appealed to her. Back in Montreal, they had a small, comfortable apartment near both of their families. Chrissie and Leonard were a loving couple, but they had very different personalities. He was an extrovert and loved to talk and to be with people. Chrissie was an introvert. Her only outgoing feature was playing her piano, which brought her so much joy. Chrissie had been given her family's piano when she married, and she happily played it every evening.

One year after they were married, Chrissie was pregnant, and Leonard's family offered them their upstairs flat with three bedrooms. The young couple was delighted with the rent—almost free! Chrissie was pleased to be close to Leonard's family, and not too far from her family. Their first daughter, Janet Anne, was named after her grandmothers: Janet (Jenny) and Annie. Janet was the first grandchild on both sides of the family and was very much loved.

In the seven years between Janet and the next daughter, Chrissie had two miscarriages, which broke her heart. She was thrilled later when baby number two, Christine (that's me!), and three years later, baby number three, Karen, both arrived safely.

Chrissie was a mum who loved to cook, bake, and sew. She had learned many Scottish recipes in her teenage years from her mother, Jenny. Chrissie liked being a housewife and often treated Leonard's mum and dad with a pie, or shortbread, or a cake that she had made. They loved her treats!

The kitchen was the main room of the house. I have an image of Karen, up in our mother's arms, with her foot resting in Mum's apron pocket as Mum got ready to bake. Janet sat at the table, grumbling as she attacked her math homework before running outside to ride her bike. I sat at the other end of the table, playing school with my little slate, waiting for Karen to join me. Chrissie often baked in the afternoon, and the house smelled of chocolate chip cookies in the oven.

Chrissie's maternal grandfather had been a tailor, and Chrissie said that his talent had been passed down to her. She loved to sew and create smocked dresses for her girls. One year, she made matching dresses for all three of us. Janet, aged 13, was not impressed being dressed like her little sisters, who were only six and three. She ranted about not wearing the dress. Chrissie refused to talk to Janet for the rest of the day. Janet got the message. Reluctantly, she wore the dress, but only for family events and not when she was with her friends.

When Janet was a baby, Leonard and his father built a cottage near a beautiful lake, Golden Lake (*Lac Doré*), in the Laurentian Mountains, north of Montreal. We would stay in the cottage all July and August. The family went swimming two or three times a day on the lake, which only allowed rowboats and canoes because of its small size. My sisters and I all became good swimmers before we were five. The family would walk around the lake most evenings. We liked to pick wild blueberries and strawberries, and Chrissie would make sweet treats on the wood stove. Sometimes Leonard would take the family fishing on the lake in a rowboat.

Leonard would come Friday nights for the weekend. Most weekends, he brought his mum, Annie, who was a widow by then. Sometimes Annie would stay for the week while Chrissie went back to Montreal with Leonard. The cottage had an outhouse, and no running water or electricity, so Chrissie was very appreciative of this and often told Annie, "Thank you for being such a good Granny. Leonard and I really enjoy the little break. It gives me a chance to visit Olive and my family. And, I can have a *bath* at home!" Annie would reply that she loved being in the country with the girls. The summers were a special time for the whole family.

From the time he was 12, Leonard had worked in a print shop and quickly became involved in their union. Leonard had been an academic child, but he had to leave school early so that he could help support his family during the Depression. When he was 40, he started a new career as an instructor of printing at a trade school. He was delighted to be an instructor. In the print shop and in the Printers' Union, he had learned a lot of French, and now he was teaching in French! He was thrilled to be called "Monsieur Le Professeur." Chrissie was very pleased with his success.

The following year, when Chrissie turned 41, they went to an International Printers' Union Convention in Philadelphia. This was a big trip for Chrissie; she loved the new experiences of taking a train, staying in a hotel, eating out in restaurants all week, and going on city tours. She was very proud of Leonard's ability to speak comfortably in front of large groups of people and loved it when people praised him.

Because Chrissie enjoyed baking, she tended to overeat and was always a little heavy. After her trip to Philadelphia in the summer of 1956, she decided to go on a diet. In November, she became ill, and by the new year, she was diagnosed with throat cancer. She could not eat without pain and soon lost a lot of weight. Leonard was devastated and told his girls to *never* go on a diet.

Chrissie's last two months of life in the late spring of 1957 were spent in bed. She and Leonard switched bedrooms with Karen and me, taking our room, which was off the kitchen where all the action was: cooking, doing homework, reading the paper, and sitting around, talking. Chrissie wanted to be near the family. Karen and I moved into our parents' bedroom, which was at the front of the house. We could hear the traffic outside and the television in the front room as we drifted off to sleep.

One day, as Chrissie lay weak in bed, she shifted her right hand in a jerking movement, and a ring flew off her emaciated finger, hitting the wastebasket with a ping. She frantically cried out to me, "Find it! It's my mother's ring. Give it to me."

When I gave her the ring, she kissed it lovingly and put it under her pillow. Almost 50 years before, Chrissie's mother had received the ruby ring from her brother as a 'remember me' gift when she left Scotland. It was passed down to Chrissie after Jenny died. Chrissie always wore her mother's ruby ring and often told the story of her uncle, a jeweller, who had made it especially for his sister, Jenny. The thought that she had possibly lost her mother's ring threw Chrissie into a panic. The ring and the piano had been Jenny's and were tactile reminders of her mother; they were, therefore, both very special.

On June 5, 1957, a date that the family would never forget, Chrissie died. Karen and I were at school, and Janet was at work. Chrissie, with Leonard and Annie by her side, quietly passed away.

Chrissie's girls were 17, 10, and 7. She had told Leonard the week before to take good care of us and not to get married again too quickly. She said, "Let your mum help you with the girls." She had been hurt when her dad married Cathy, someone she did not like, so soon after Jenny had died. She wanted to protect her daughters from that same upsetting experience.

Chrissie had just turned 42, had been married for 19 years, and had three daughters, whom she loved very much. Her father, brother Tom, Aunt Mary, cousin Nancy, and friend Olive had all visited her a week or so before she died; they were all there for her at the end. And so, Chrissie, loving mother, wife, daughter, sister, niece, cousin, and friend, was gone too soon.

CHRISSIE (FAR RIGHT), 1953, GOLDEN LAKE COTTAGE

Author Reflection - Christine Norris
North Vancouver, BC, Canada

It has always been painful to spend time thinking about my mother. Many years ago, I was taking a university course and working on a presentation with two other students. One was a florist who talked about flowers. The other was a nurse who talked about patients dying and dealing with their families. Initially, I was a little impatient because they were off topic, but suddenly it felt like a lightning bolt had struck me, and I started crying. I couldn't stop for two days.

After I stopped crying and was able to process this, I had two realizations. It hit me why I was never a flower lover. I always thought I was allergic to them, but I suddenly remembered I had never seen many flowers until my mother's funeral—there were mountains of them. I realized that I was not allergic to flowers, but worse still, I associated flowers with death. The other realization I had was that I was 42, the same age my mother was when she died.

Fifty years after our mother died, my sisters and I met in Montreal. We had a family gathering at her church. Olive, our mum's friend, was there, still lively at age 92. I often think of a photo I have of Mum and Olive as teenagers, side by side. Who would predict that one would die at age 42 and the other at age 97?

In 2013, it was the 75th anniversary of my parents' wedding. To celebrate the event, I scanned dozens of old pictures and made a photo book for my sisters and me. We all agree that it is a beautiful keepsake.

Each event, including writing my mother's story, has been an emotional event. But the very positive result is that I remember more and more about my dear mother, Chrissie Law, who was taken from her family far too soon.

10 | Jennifer Juniper Angeli's Story of Emma

I am writing to you and about you on my birthday. My first birthday with my daughter. I am surely blessed. Where do I start? I just want to tell you I miss you. You would like Sapphire Mignon. When she smiles at me, my heart explodes and all is perfect. All is as it should be. How did you feel when I was born? Niña and I found the letters you kept when you and Tim first met. Love letters, definitely crazy, young, idealistic and madly in love.

Your world was open, so full of possibilities, travelling, music, art. Side by side with your eternal love. Were you disappointed you had children in your first years of marriage? Any regrets? Did you disappear a little bit? Did you fulfill any of your dreams?

Emma Marie Gioacchini. Born in Boston, Massachusetts, October 1, 1941. Parents: Carolina Anna Maria Tauro and Americo Flavio Gioacchini. Immigrants from Italy. The youngest of six—three boys and three girls. The only one born in a hospital. A Catholic family (but you could never understand confession, you said, so you started making them up and eventually turned against organized religion altogether).

What was your childhood like? In your high school annual, you were voted "the girl with the most interesting clothing combinations." You were close to Dolly, your sister, gabbing all the time, laughing, finishing each other's sentences. You were close to Grampi, your Pop. There were always instruments around, and Grampi was always playing, drinking the wine he made in the basement, friends over, a lively atmosphere. Music and dancing. Your mom, Nonni, *never* drank. She only ever had one sip of champagne on her wedding night. She was quiet until she'd had enough, and then would let it be known.

Who did you take after? Were you the lively social party girl, or the quiet one who sat and watched? I remember a bit of both. It seemed rare that you drank, but when you did, you were happy and lively, cheering to all and everything. Cheers lamp! Cheers floor! Cheers lightbulb! Mostly you would sit back and watch all of the goings on with a smile on your face and a rock in your sit. Enjoying the atmosphere, throwing out a zinger comment every now and then, sometimes fierce but never malicious, and always with a knowing and wise laugh behind it.

You were definitely a mother. You felt like a mother, Mom. Although when I was little, you seemed distant, maybe not sure if this was the life you wanted, maybe wanting to escape?

After high school, you went to The Pennsylvania Academy of Art. You loved drawing and painting. You worked as a librarian's assistant in the art/music section, which gave you a high appreciation for classical music. You worked very hard at losing your Bostonian accent. You said you never wanted to be identified from any one place.

You didn't finish; you went back to live with your parents in Lynn, Massachusetts. Why? Your sister Dolly had two children, and you helped with the babysitting. That's where you met Tim. He lived beside Dolly. Tim was attending the Boston Museum Academy of Art, and you met at one of his all-night Greek music love fests. You got to know each other, similar likes and dislikes, same ideals and thoughts about the world and its politics. And you fell in love. Tim was 19, and you 23.

This was 1965. The year of the love letters. The Vietnam War was heating up. Friends were being drafted. Tim was *not* going to go, fully supported by you. You stayed in Boston, trying to make money for your future together, while Tim worked on a dude ranch in Colorado. And this is where the correspondence really took off: planning your life together, professing your undying and eternal love, planning your escape if the draft board came after Tim. Two love crazed idealistic people who just wanted to be together side by side, painting, playing music, travelling the world, each other's muses, surrounded by the great chance of war that could dash their dreams and lives forever.

You got a job at a radio station for classical music as a programming coordinator. But then turned it down to move to Colorado and marry Tim. You married on December 14, 1965. You lived in a small cabin in the woods. 'Uncle' Charlie's cabin. He was dead. One morning you woke up with blue paint smeared by a man's hands all over your body, not a speck on Tim or the sheets.

It was getting harder to feel free with the impending draft hanging over Tim's head, so you fled to Nova Scotia and lived in an apartment and then the garage in Tim's family's summer home. You were only in the apartment for a couple of months when you conceived Niña. That night you said you saw two little faerie-like girls coming up the stairs to your apartment. Meanwhile, this 'draft-dodging' was *not* okay with Tim's family. So, after being shamed and blackmailed by his parents into doing his duty as an American, you returned. Tim turned himself in, and by some extraordinary fluke, the government sent him the wrong orders, which temporarily excused him. Pregnant with Niña, you moved to New Haven, Connecticut, where your sister Dolly now lived. Niña was born, December 27, 1966. Sixteen months later, I was born, April 30, 1968.

You said it was very eerie and uncomfortable for Tim, with so few young men around, always the questions and disapproving glances. You decided to move to Canada, since you liked the politics there. We moved back to Boston to stay with Nonni…your pop had died shortly after Niña was born. Then you, Tim, Dolly, Niña, and Nor went to Montreal to find a job. I stayed with Nonni and Kyle.

Though both Tim and Dolly found jobs right away, you hated Montreal. You found it dark and cold, and the divide between the English and French was very palpable. You went back to Boston to make alternate plans. We settled on Toronto, though the place you really wanted to live was British Columbia. You heard of the wilderness and freedom there. We lived in Toronto until September of 1971.

Then, our family, with two other families, decided to leave. Our destination: British Columbia. So, five kids, five adults, two dogs and six cats got in a station wagon with U-Haul and drove across Canada to find a plot of land on which to grow our own food.

We ended up on a 14-acre wooded property we bought for $7,000, seven miles up a dirt road in a district called Black Creek. Tim built our house sans electricity or plumbing, and you grew a garden. We had goats, ducks, geese, chickens, dogs, and at one point 16 cats (until you freaked out one day, and we had to take most of them to the dump with one can of sardines to fend for themselves), guinea pigs, rabbits and two horses. We also built on our land, with the help of other searchers and expatriates, a geodesic dome, a cabin, a teepee, and a treehouse. Needless to say, there were always new sleeping bags to wake up to.

Somehow, the Jehovah Witnesses would always find our place. And one time, they came all dressed in their Sunday best, knocked on the door, and you opened it, naked and smiling. And you, always the gracious host, invited them in for tea.

You and Tim had an open relationship for a while. Whose idea was that? You fell in love with him and left us. We were in Colorado, and you hopped the bus home to be with him. It was in Boise, Idaho, that you made the choice to come back. My very clear image as I ran past the door was you sitting naked on the bed with Tim and crying. Was it harder to leave us or harder to come back?

Both you and Tim taught me to stand up for what I believe in. And you led by example when you took the School Board to court so Niña and I didn't have to go. Eventually, when we decided to give school a try, our lifestyle became more settled.

Tim made custom jewellery and continued with his art, and you supported him, doing the books, making jewellery yourself, taking various cooking jobs. But what about your art? You were a beautiful drawer and painter. Were any of your dreams being fulfilled?

Eventually, you found a great group of women and did the illustrations for women's support books that your friend had written, and also pursued your love of photography. And you were always there for our large extended family. Did you know three of our dearest friends felt you were their best friend, and I'm sure if I asked a number of others, they'd say the same? I wonder if you were aware of the impact you had on so many people's lives?

You weren't the typical mom. There weren't a lot of sit-down meals prepared. Though you made sure we had our daily dose of peanut butter, garlic, cayenne pepper, and tons of Vitamin C. Keeping us clean certainly wasn't a priority, nor was a set bedtime. When we were in our teens and wanted to try acid and mushrooms, you said fine, though you preferred we were at home so you could make sure we were okay. Sex, too, was fine, but again, if we were home you knew we were safe. In the end, I think your way worked.

I look at my daughter Sapphire and her baby brother River and wonder if I can be that open and free with them. All I know is you gave me a safe and supportive place to think and grow, and always with the utmost respect. It's funny; as I write this, I find I'm only thinking of the good stuff. I wonder if you were alive today, if I would have any issues with you.

In 1987, a year after I left home, they found the brain tumour. You had to move from your peaceful, quiet home in the woods to an unfamiliar, empty house in town. And you hated it. I hear from friends you were scared, but you never told me or talked to me about your fears. Did you try?

After the operation, you lost a lot of vision and became very dependent on Tim, a struggle for you both, but you made sure to see my plays, always so supportive. I was Grusha in *The Caucasian Chalk Circle*, and you loved it. I remember seeing you in the audience and noticing you had your eyes closed. How bad was your vision? We never talked about it. You were changed, scared, timid (you could never be considered timid before). You carried now an unsure-ness with you. Your great verve for life diminished, though your amazing spark was still there.

Two in the morning, Tim called, choked out the words "Emma is dying." Taken to the hospital in Victoria. He asked if I wanted to see you before they took you off life support. I said no, I didn't want that to be my last image of you. Did that hurt your feelings? I've always wondered. Tim said he felt a powerful energy enter him as you were dying in his arms at home in the bathroom. You had just come back from an evening walk with Tim and Judy, our dog.

We were just getting reconnected again. I felt I was just getting interested in you again, wanting to know about your life, your childhood, your dreams, your thoughts. I feel ripped-off.

When I dream about you, are you stopping by to say "Hi"? You always have a big smile on your face and give me a hug, and then off you go.

EMMA, 1986, COURTENAY, BC, JENNIFER'S GRADUATION

Author Reflection - Jennifer Juniper Angeli
Vancouver, BC, Canada

I find myself in this reflection, writing again, directly to you. It was not my intent. It just feels right to me. To write 'about' you feels too impersonal, too distant. You are always close by. Whether I carry you in me or you are just part of life all around. I continue to reflect daily, year after year, and I breathe...

How apropos; it is Mother's Day, and here I am reflecting and writing about you. I passed the milestone seven years ago; I became older than you were when you died. I held my breath on that day. One of your best friends sent me a thoughtful and poignant text acknowledging that milestone. She too had been holding her breath. Texts, I think you would have loved them. I think you would have had tons of fun creating your very own emoji. You would have totally gotten into sending texts to your daughters and grandchildren and getting an instant reply—just a short "Hi" with a myriad of interesting and fun emojis attached. Just to feel connected. I think so anyway.

It has been now 17 years since I wrote your story. Sapphire is 17, and River is 12. Life carries on. I have two half-sisters. It is such a strange thing to process. If you hadn't died, these two young women would not be here. If you had lived, maybe my children would not be here. It all becomes a great big mess in my mind; a reflection on life and the hugeness of it all and of life's twists.

And here we are, life evolving, time dancing on. You are still so very missed by so many who adored you. They miss your deep soul, your friendship, and how you chose to 'be' in this world. What do I reflect on? A full adult life without you? That is a lot. It's all just wonder and conjecture anyway. A missing of what could have been in the numerous possible realities.

But really, all that is real is a missing of you. Just you.

I thought that you would like to know that the name Emma became the number one baby girl name in North America from 2014 to 2019 and has been in the top 5 since 2003. That, you would have found to be the most hysterical of all!

11 | Janyne Sinclair's Story of Ruth

I wish I knew more about my mother. However, close to sixty-six years after her passing, Ruth King Yates is but fragments in my memory. And unfortunately, there are no other family members alive to provide information, answer questions, or fill in some of the many gaps.

My mom, Ruth King, was born to Gertrude and Sanford King on September 28, 1916, in Guelph, Ontario. Mom grew up in Guelph with her two sisters, Joyce and Edith, and the family English Springer Spaniel dog. I'm not sure if her sisters were older or younger, but for some reason, in my mind's eye, Mom was the middle child.

I have little information about my mom between her birth and marriage. Even the photos I managed to find are all from her adulthood. I don't recall hearing much about Mom's parents, but I know she connected well with her two sisters, who were both married with families. They all wrote letters to each other regularly, and I remember going with Mom on a train trip to Ontario when I was very small. I'm not aware why I lacked exposure to and knowledge of Mom's family. I surmise it was primarily the distance factor.

I assume Mom finished high school, and she had told me about her nurse's training during World War II. I have a photo of her in her graduation gown in front of brick buildings, but I don't know the name of the training school. It's likely that she worked as a nurse after graduation (but again, I'm not sure where) until she met my dad, Bill Yates.

Dad was a classic tall, dark, and handsome guy who sometimes sported a moustache. He was in the Royal Canadian Air Force (RCAF) training for service in WWII. I don't know when they met or how long they dated. They married in Guelph in 1942 when Mom was 26. They took a short honeymoon in Vancouver, then Mom went back to Guelph (possibly spending some of that time living with her family), while Dad returned to his post in the RCAF until the war ended. I have a sweet photo album that Mom put together and sent to Dad while he was overseas, containing homey photos and loving, flirty comments.

When the war ended, Mom and Dad moved to Alberta. They set up a first home in one of the rental cabins at the Hollowood Store, located west of Cochrane on what was then the #1 Highway to Banff. Mom became a housewife, and my dad found work on oil drilling rigs.

I was their first child, born in the winter of 1946, when Mom was thirty. My paternal Granny told me that I came into the world with much difficulty and that my mom nearly died having me. I never did learn exactly what that meant, whether this was literal or somehow more figurative.

I was born with a partial cleft palate, which made feeding complicated. Mom's training and nursing experience gave her the problem-solving skills and competency to tend to my early medical needs. I have a memory from when I was a toddler of being in hospital after corrective cleft palate surgery and Mom visiting me daily at suppertime so she could give me my antibiotic injection. She would pinch my skin hard so I'd notice the needle less.

After the surgery, Mom took me to speech therapy and encouraged me to practice. I can only imagine how difficult this may have been at that time when there was a great deal of shame surrounding birth defects of any kind. It was likely kept a secret, as there was no mention of it in an otherwise very detailed baby book. I speculate that Mom may have been depressed.

Mom and Dad had friends among the oil rig workers and their families, many of whom comprised a mobile community of workers travelling to where the work was, all around southern Alberta. I recall hearing that we had lived in Drayton Valley, Two Hills, Three Hills, and Mundare, before settling in Devon. There we lived in a small trailer, then in an apartment at the front of a company warehouse.

Mom and Dad enjoyed house parties and social drinking; Mom smoked cigarettes, and Dad smoked a pipe and cigars, usually the small 'cigarillos'. They loved each other; I could see that they laughed a lot and liked to sing together. My parents had occasional arguments too—and once a big upset when Dad was teaching Mom to drive and she drove into a roadside ditch!

By the time I was in grade two and as I grew, Mom and I began to have power struggles and loud arguments on occasion (she was the one who administered discipline). I was willful and would yell, "You can't tell me what to do!" I wish I could remember what she said back. Makes me wonder what it was like for her to have such a little handful.

Mom was warm and soft and laughed easily. She had brown hair, hazel eyes, and wore glasses and a watch on a chain around her neck. She was 5 feet, 5 inches, a bit on the heavy side, and always wore dresses, adding a hat and gloves for church. I remember her sitting at her dresser to get ready to go out. She would comb and style her hair, put on pretty jewellery (like her opal earrings and matching pendant) and apply modest cosmetics. Mom did not wear nail polish or a lot of makeup.

Mom really thrived in social settings. She enjoyed people, sang in the Anglican Church choir, and was good at organizing gatherings like tea and birthday parties, as well as picnics. She belonged to an Around the World Shopping Club—a club that mailed beautiful artifacts from a foreign land direct to members each month for about $2 each, postpaid and duty-free. One of the items in Mom's collection was a ceramic bottle containing water from the River Jordan! Club members took turns hosting tea parties with fancy cups and saucers and ate finger food while they reviewed their treasures.

As I got older, Mom recognized I was shy and she encouraged me to reach out to meet other children, which I was reluctant to do. She would hold my head when I threw up. She cared and comforted me when I got the mumps and measles, treated my miscellaneous bumps and scrapes and soothed me when I felt unhappy. I knew what it was like to feel loved and cared for.

My brother David was born in May of 1953. Fortunately, his birth was uncomplicated and he was healthy. I speculate that Mom and Dad must have been relieved.

My mom was a good cook; her roast beef with Yorkshire Pudding was my favourite meal. She also made great cakes, always with icing and decorations. She kept our homes clean and tidy, perhaps because we were often in small spaces. There was big excitement when Dad got a job with a new company, and he bought us a house in Calgary.

Sometime after we had moved from Devon to Calgary, Mom auditioned for a radio contest, singing *Dear Little Boy of Mine*. She did not win, but was excited about it nonetheless. I still have a warped 78 rpm recording of that performance.

We spent lots of family time together in the car, especially Sunday drives and picnics. Mom made picnic meals, including egg salad sandwiches, potato salad, tea in a Thermos bottle, and cake or pudding desserts. I remember one magical night, we stopped and all got out of the car to look up at the sky filled with billions of stars.

My childhood summers were spent with my paternal grandparents at 'the farm'—a cattle ranch near Cochrane, Alberta. I loved those summers and enjoyed 'helping' (i.e. watching) Granny cook and do household chores. I would follow Grandpa Jack to the barn and the garage to watch his chores too.

I think I was in grade two when Dad bought me a horse of my own. I named him Brownie and was in heaven riding him for the couple of years we were together. I have no idea what Mom and Dad and David did during those summers, but they always came to pick me up in plenty of time to shop for September school supplies when we got back home.

My Granny (my paternal grandmother) once told me that Mom said to her that she "knew she would not live to raise her kids" and, in that case, she wanted Granny to raise us. This information was only shared with me as a statement and was not for discussion.

Mom took lots of pictures and made albums for both my brother and me so we would have memories. Unfortunately, many years later, when Granny's house was sold, the trunks containing this and other memorabilia disappeared. A whole section of Mom's life was somehow left behind.

Mom's life changed drastically one morning when I was in grade four. I found Mom partly dressed in her slip, lying on the floor next to her dressing table. I didn't know what was happening, but I did know we needed help and ran next door to get the neighbour. She came right away; we managed to push Mom up on the bed somehow, and then an ambulance came. After that, I can recall only fragments of memories about what happened, or in what order.

It turned out that event was a stroke. Afterwards, Mom remained in the hospital except for two visits home in a wheelchair. She died from brain cancer later in 1956 at Holy Cross Hospital in Calgary. She was thirty-nine years old, and I turned nine that November.

I've missed her ever since.

RUTH ON HER WEDDING DAY, 1942, GUELPH, ONTARIO

Author Reflection - Janyne Sinclaire
Nanaimo, BC, Canada

It has been over 65 years since my mom passed. I may not have a coherent recall of my life with her and all my perceptions of her, but I have myself as a reflection of her. She loved me and raised me for eight years, so much about her can be gleaned from observations of my life. From her, I learned the values of kindness, respect, precision, quality, and laughter. And, also, I learned the importance of hanging my clothes on the hanger with hooks all facing the same direction in case of an emergency evacuation!

My mom modelled love and commitment, the ability to cry, and also how to stand up and talk back. When I was in the hospital and/or under medical treatments, she advocated for me. She recognized my sensitivity and soothed me as much as possible despite my bouts of contrariness. Because of her, I know in my bones what it feels like to be loved.

To find a photo of her, I needed to dig through boxes of old photos that hadn't been disturbed since they landed in my garage in 2001. As I gathered pictures of Mom and Dad from their courtship and wedding, along with those of my childhood era, I felt nostalgia and some enjoyment. However, my feelings soon turned to sadness about what I've missed and the emptiness of being without a family.

Why do I have so much trouble trying to remember my mom? Well, I guess that despite therapy, I have not yet completely resolved the experience that I think of as the end of my childhood: Mom's stroke, her cancer diagnosis, and subsequent death soon after. Three years later, my father died suddenly, adding another layer of trauma and resulting in a move for my brother and me from Saskatchewan to Calgary to live with Granny and Jack—our paternal grandparents.

I think I was in 'freeze' mode for most of my adult life, from age thirteen until my mid-fifties, when I began to learn about Adverse

Childhood Experiences and unresolved trauma. Fortunately, in the early 1990s, I found a good therapist for ongoing support.

As I come to the completion of this story, I recognize there is value in the process of calling forth these memories, however troublesome they feel. I have survived. All that I went through gave me grounds for compassion towards others and fuelled my career choices.

I am grateful.

12 | James Edgington's Story of Jennifer

My mother only had 23 years of life. She passed away following a car accident, in what we call a 'snowy Bolton', in the north of England in January of 1985. I was 14 months old and literally have no memories of her. I'm piecing Mum together here from other people's memories, as I have done all my life.

My father has given me a great sense of who she was and has always been open to answering my questions about her. Mum's mum—my grandma—had also been a source of information providing other details about Mum. However, in May 2020, during the COVID-19 pandemic, grandma died.

While sorting through her flat after her passing, I discovered photo albums I'd never seen, including many of Mum growing up and a book my mother had written as a school assignment. Mum must have been around 10 or 11 when writing this book. It has a sketch of her on the front cover with her name and the title, "The Story of My Life."

Born on June 10, 1961, in Bolton, England, Jennifer Margaret Cave describes the day as miserable and dreary, writing, "perhaps not helped by the fact that I was to be born then."

This felt so negative and depressing, and so contrary to stories I'd been told about my mum's positivity, happy smile, and energy. I knew there had been tension between Mum and my Aunty Judith. What I didn't expect was the way my mother went on to write about how she weighed 9 pounds 9 ounces at birth, "unlike my weakling of a sister who had weighed a mere 6 pounds 4 ounces," when she was born in October, 1956.

I was getting a sense that my mum didn't mince her words, and I liked it. Clearly a strong-minded person, my mother goes on to describe memories in her life that had a huge impact on her during her early years.

Mum describes one of her earliest memories of a time when she said goodbye to her sister at the front door, turned around only to trip and cut her forehead on the corner of the couch. This section was incredibly detailed with the pain she recalled. She describes the "unseemly plaster" a doctor put over her cut and that her father had given her Liquorice Allsorts for being "good and patient."

Her sense of self is fascinating, writing at a young age about her life experiences as if she was elderly and writing a memoir. Not only does the book detail her experiences as a young girl, it also describes a recurring dream she had in which she caused the accident of falling over and cutting her head.

Mum describes her first caravan trip at age three. It doesn't sound like it was a great experience; her mother and father weren't keen on the outdoor elements of a holiday in a caravan, but it gave Mum enough lasting memories to be included in her life story. She writes about the whole family being together on the trip, including her grandma.

At three years old, Mum started at a nursery school where her older sister attended as a pupil in the primary school. Mum didn't want to be there; she screamed and cried at being dropped off, but eventually her mum would tear herself away and let the nursery staff take over.

Knowing her big sister was in the same building, she would also scream for Judith, who had to be brought out of lessons on a few occasions to provide a familiar face. There is no mention in my mother's self-penned life story of a happy time at the nursery; she didn't want to be there.

Mum describes in detail how the children were meant to sleep in the afternoon. She didn't want to. "We all had to climb into silly little beds," she writes and goes on to say, "I cried, screamed, and shouted so that all the children that wanted to go to sleep couldn't." This made me giggle. A personality that I never knew came to life but was so familiar to me because it's probably something I would have done as well. Mum describes a teacher at infant school who "did not understand my temperament" and had "no sympathy whatsoever in any of my many troubles."

Mum experienced bereavement at around four or five years old, describing how her grandad died. Mum candidly writes that she didn't understand properly and was not upset, confessing that she didn't really remember him but felt empathy towards her Grandma, who missed him terribly at the time.

The next chapter in Mum's book was tough—her dad died, and she had a second experience of grief in childhood. Mum described how he had been ill for some time and passed away on March 1, 1969. Mum was only seven and yet still recognized that her mum "bore the whole weight on her shoulders." Mum says this changed her whole life, and that she didn't cry, staying strong for her mum and sister.

This maturity and resilience at seven was overwhelming to me; I was in awe of this child I was reading about. Mum felt a duty to her dad as she was hopeful that he would return from hospital. Her dad's last words to her were, "Help your Mum, Jen, until I come back." So, Mum also felt a duty to remain hopeful that he would return from hospital. This pain, juxtaposed with the love she felt for her dad, was incredible, and she responded with more sensitivity towards her mum.

The next pages relay her emotional journey of bereavement with details of blame, anger, uncertainty, and her commitment to get on with life. These gave me insight into how much my grandad loved his family and how much he was loved in return.

Continuing with her story, Mum describes how life had to carry on and she talks about her guinea pig, Tingaling, named after a dog from a TV series the family watched faithfully called *The Forsythe Saga*. I have an urge to find the old repeats of it just to connect with what my mum would have watched at the time. Mum describes how her Tingaling died and she cried, all the while thinking that anyone reading her story would think she was heartless for crying at this and not the death of her own father.

Mum writes about moving to senior school and attending Bolton School around age nine—the school she attended while writing this assignment. To people outside of Greater Manchester, the school is held in high regard with an impressive history in the town and alumni, including Sir Ian McKellen. Mum wrote about liking English and drama but mainly looking forward to the weekend when she would visit her uncle's farm in Penrith, about 90 miles north of Bolton. I vaguely knew of the family connection to this area from my grandma, but it seemed to be really special to my mum.

Mum wrote about the various farm animals with stories that featured the feral cats born in the barn—of which there is a picture of her holding two—and the farm dog having puppies. Mum described how she had always wanted a dog, but her mum had been wary from her own bad experience with them. I don't remember Grandma having pets or being very fond of them because of the mess, but Mum managed to get her puppy at the end of that weekend. She had to make the difficult decision of whether to name it Kip or Scamp... "I finally decided on Scamp."

Scamp becomes a rather large focus of the story at this point, Mum writing of how beautiful he looked when he was sleeping and how mischievous he was and would do things like pull the tablecloth off the table and sit on it. If a dog's personality could match a human temperament, Mum and Scamp seemed to be a match.

Mum goes on to talk about the end of her first year at Bolton School. She mentions other girls in her class who separately had passions for football, ballet, horses, books, and music. "I still enjoyed drama and singing and loved to act in plays," she goes on, "however my chief aim and ambition was to become a veterinary surgeon." I had discovered her fire and passion for myself.

Her story nearly over, Mum only mentions this time of her life as coming "down to earth" after holidays with the euphoria of being away, to face revision for exams. She was 11.

Moving away from the story Mum wrote about herself, I consider how the description of her has been created for me by other people. My father is the main source of information about Mum's adult life. I know from him that after Mum finished school, she attended Manchester Metropolitan University to study food technology—at what was known as the Toast Rack campus. Dad told me a story of her coming home and insisting from that moment on they would only ever eat free-range eggs because she'd studied a documentary about caged chickens and was repulsed.

Mum and Dad were high school sweethearts. They both attended an Amateur Dramatics group where they were involved in many productions over the years. Performing was a hobby, a passion, and as well as something they had done professionally for a period of time. Mum and Dad married in Bolton in 1980. In an old VHS tape and photo album of their wedding, Mum is a beautiful, blonde, slim woman with a beaming smile. Mum wanted a large family, and I was the first of many planned, born in autumn of 1983.

Dad told me both the fairy tale version of Mum as well as stories of the real woman, like how she was reluctant to get up early—so much so, that she would duck out of the early morning bottle feedings that I demanded as a baby.

Mum and Dad never argued; Dad was always careful to say they 'had words.' Apparently, Mum had a temper that many other people had not been privy to. Dad remembered a time when they 'had words' in the kitchen of their old house and Mum had kicked the oven in anger.

Because I never knew what my mum had wanted for me, something special Dad told me that has stuck with me—the instructions she'd given Dad when I was born. Mum had grown up getting nothing but hand-me-downs from her sister. She categorically did not want me to have anything second hand.

Mum was involved in a traffic accident in a 'snowy Bolton' in January, 1985. I was in the car, in a baby seat, and Dad told me that I had blood on me when I was found by the ambulance crew. They thought it was from Mum touching me after the accident. Dad has always told me that she must have turned around to check that I was okay before passing out and going into a coma. Mum died on January 30, 1985, at Salford Royal Hospital.

Mum's final words in her book were, "At this rate, we will be leaving school before we can say Jack Robinson." Although it might sound like a cliché, the stark reality is that life is short. In her case, it truly was. That final, foreboding statement stays with me now because, in reality, it described her life.

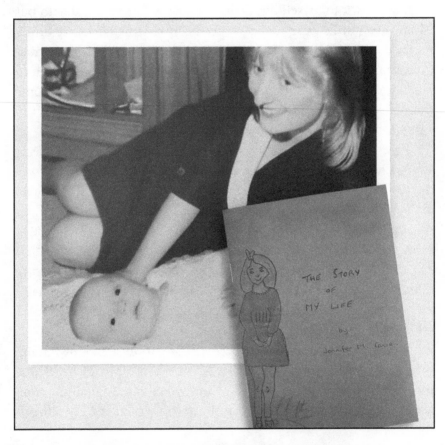

JENNIFER AND JAMES, 1983, BOLTON ENGLAND

Author Reflection - James Edgington
Bolton, England, UK

Reflecting on loss without memory is a bizarre notion, but nevertheless that has been my lived experience. Writing my mother's story and reading it back to myself highlighted that I will never be able to put Mum dying at 23 years old into perspective. It had, and continues to have, a huge impact on me, even though I don't remember experiencing it. She was so young, and I had only just made it into her story. Memories of my mum have been formed by other people throughout my life, and it's only more recently in my mid-thirties that I have really processed these thoughts and descriptions.

I grew up knowing that my mum was no longer with me. It wasn't strange for me to have one parent; it wasn't a new experience; it was matter of fact. As I matured and visited friends with two parents or had to respond to teachers who would say things like, "When Mummy picks you up," or "When Mummy gets your lunch ready," it hit me. Mummy wasn't there. I was also sensitive to the fact that I was extremely similar to my dad, but on the flip side, I was very different as well. I had certain personality and physical traits that I didn't recognize in him and realized that these were of my mum. I cried many times, but that was later.

Dad was my primary source of information about my mum, being my memory of her by proxy. My relationship with my dad is incredibly close. I am an only child and speak with him all the time about her, even though I'm sure at times this was incredibly difficult for him.

Finding the school assignment Mum wrote at essentially the same time as embarking on *My Mother's Story* was a gift that I could have only dreamed of. It gave me a real sense of who she was as a girl. I knew some things about her, but this was my mum candidly writing about her ambitions, and I felt I had a newfound sense of her soul.

The other place in her book that gave me great pause for introspection was when Mum wrote that she was 'troubled'. I wondered if this had been read today by a teacher at school, what questions would have been asked. What were her troubles? And how did she know her own temperament at such a young age? I'm still learning mine and I'm pushing forty.

Reading about Mum and her dog was touching. She loved Scamp, and it was through her description, I realized, that this was as close to a memory of her love that I was going to get. It was an overwhelming feeling that I connected with deeply. Love is something we can't physically see; we feel it; we sense it. Because I could not possibly recall experiencing her love, this sentence in the story touched me in a way that felt familiar and comforting.

I often wonder what my mum might think about issues in the world today. From her book she appears head strong, loving, and opinionated—traits I have definitely inherited. Revisiting the story that Dad told me of when Mum kicked the oven was not only hilarious but made me cry because it reminded me that this was the first time I had heard of Mum losing her temper, something I was really prone to doing when I was younger. It was through these stories that I felt like I had found her, found my connection, and realized that I had been lost.

All in all, this process has been a cathartic one. Sharing this story with the other authors has also been therapeutic, as I've felt that, as much as we've told stories on a common theme, it's all so unique and subjective, and we all process these events in a different way. I've always been relatively devoid of emotional reaction on the subject and talked quite openly about Mum, but if I do get upset, it takes me off guard.

I realized I've been on a mission most of my life to make my mum even more real to me, and writing my mother's story has made that possible.

13 | Soma Keo's Story of Solarie

Solarie Som was born on August 2, 1950, in Kompong Cham, Cambodia. She was the first child of eight to Iv Srun Som and Chhun Huoy Luch, who had an arranged marriage—an ancient tradition. Solarie's father worked in customs and her mother was a businesswoman. Solarie was educated in a French curriculum from a young age, as Cambodia was a French colony until 1953, and the language continued to be a strong influence into the 1990s. She grew up in Kompong Cham through her childhood and teenage years until she attended the University in Phnom Penh to study and become a pharmacist. In 1973, Solarie married her first husband, Kim Chun Eap, at the age of 23.

Upon graduating from University at the age of 26, Solarie opened a pharmacy with her parents' support. But just two short years later, her life was turned upside down. In 1975, the Communist Khmer Rouge seized power and forced Cambodians of all ages into slavery. The brutal regime's official policy was to dismantle the nuclear family.

Solarie's parents and two of her sisters died from execution, starvation, and overwork, respectively. Her first husband was also killed when the Khmer Rouge forced city residents to relocate to concentration camps in the countryside to work as farmers, digging canals, and tending to crops. Solarie and her remaining siblings were also forcibly separated from one another.

Despite the civil war lasting nearly five years, somehow Solarie managed to escape the camps with her four surviving siblings and their spouses. Solarie survived because she was a fighter and never gave up. She always took care of her younger siblings and became 'the parent.' Her silence spoke volumes as deep fears and years of brutality left her scarred and unwilling to speak about those times and the memories she wished to bury.

In December 1980, Solarie arrived in Montreal to join her younger sister, who had arrived a few weeks prior, with her husband and their newborn daughter. Since Cambodia was a French colony and her immediate family already spoke the language, Montreal was a sensible choice.

Solarie amended her age in official Canadian documents, believing being two years younger would be necessary for an entry age cut-off to study in Quebec, to practice there someday as a pharmacist. In hindsight, it turned out to be unnecessary as she instead became a business owner to alleviate the financial burden of having to start her new life as an immigrant. This would also become a source of confusion for the remainder of her life... how old was she, really?

My mom was petite at 5'0" and looked stylish without trying too hard. Her black hair was always permed, and she drove a French sports car while in University. Growing up, Mom enjoyed sewing clothes for herself and her whole family. She also loved to put on makeup and get dolled up.

Along with a change in priorities, her move to Canada in 1980 also caused a night and day shift in Mom's personality and appearance (for more reasons than seeing snow for the first time in her life in Montreal!). She was now more concerned about becoming a businesswoman, supporting her family, and making long-term financial goals—although her love for brand names and designer bags did not change—whenever she could afford it.

Mom partnered with her younger sister's family to operate a convenience store below the duplex building where they lived. In 1982, a man by the name of Sothearo came to visit his older sister Mo, who also lived in Montreal. Mom knew Sothearo from Cambodia because his older brother Peou was friends with one of Mom's brothers. Sothearo and Mom started a romantic affair, despite her siblings' dismay. Perhaps they weren't fond of him because of his stubborn personality and the fact that he was younger than Mom. Her involvement with him would change the dynamics and interfere with the 'power structure' of the family.

Furthermore, two of Mom's brothers would end up working for Sothearo later on, where boundaries and expectations got complicated for all the parties involved. Nonetheless, Mom and Sothearo—my dad—were married in 1984. She worked very hard to provide for her siblings, continuing to instill the same financial drive when it came to starting her own family.

A year later, Mom gave birth to me (prematurely) at age 35 (or was it 37?) before returning to work within a week, as she was the only employee at the store. Four years after my birth, she had her second child in 1989, my brother Amarith. Mom was now too busy when I was in grade one, so she sent me to boarding school in downtown Montreal.

I remember spending some days with my mom at the convenience store, sitting behind the counter and sipping on coffee when I was only eight or so. Sometimes, Mom would let me suck on sugar cubes. Ironically, I was never curious enough to open a chocolate bar, nor was I ever offered one.

Mom's sister's family decided to move to the suburbs for other work opportunities and they decided to sell the convenience store in 1992. A year later, Mom and Dad invested in a Dunkin' Donuts franchise.

The following four years flew by quickly as my parents both worked tirelessly. Mom became a seamstress, since it was a skill she had from a young age, while Dad was busy running the donut franchise.

In 1996, my parents sold that franchise, packed up and moved to British Columbia after visiting their family friend who would later become a business partner. This was our family's final move, where my parents decided to invest in a different franchise restaurant and business ventures and where our family would settle and start a new life.

Our first family home was a rental in Burnaby until we moved to West Vancouver in 1998 to be closer to the business, where my parents eventually bought a house. Although she grew up Buddhist, when we first moved to West Vancouver, Mom and our family were welcomed into a local Catholic church and were baptized. This made us feel like part of the community. Being in a new neighbourhood where everyone spoke English and being unsure of her own English made it a challenge for Mom to attend social events or make friends locally. She loved hosting parties occasionally for friends and family who visited from out of town, spending hours in the kitchen to prepare elaborate Cambodian meals.

Eventually Mom did teach herself English, but for a long time it seemed like she pretended to not speak it that well, either because it was easier or perhaps she was shy. Over the years, Mom started to enjoy her life a little bit more, having more spare time for hands-on things she enjoyed: sewing, gardening, cooking, and travelling back to Southeast Asia. She found a purpose as a stay-at-home mom, whether it was reupholstering furniture or renovating the house, she was resourceful in learning any new skill. It amazes me how much she did, as well as being the glue that held the family together.

Our mom ensured that she passed on the same Cambodian values that she had growing up to both my brother and I. We learned the value of a higher education and my brother inherited her culinary mindset, as he can recreate any dish from scratch.

A proper lady in the eyes of Cambodian society did not laugh too loudly or walk too quickly. Generations of rural Cambodian girls were taught traditional rules in the classroom for how to be a 'proper woman', dutiful wife and homemaker. Mom often commented on the way I laughed or when I was being too loud. She was quite strict with me throughout my teenage rebellion years. I'm the one who caused her a lot of grey hairs, but also the one who pulled them out for her.

When Amarith graduated from Vancouver College in 2007, Mom did not join us for the ceremony, as she was in Asia secretly seeing doctors. We found out later Mom was diagnosed with a chronic hepatitis B infection (HBV) and, after unsuccessful treatments in BC, she sought Chinese medicinal herbal remedies in Asia. We are still unsure of how she contracted it, however. HBV infection can be associated with the risk of non-liver cancers, especially digestive system cancers.

Back in Vancouver, and sometime during the second week of July 2007, Mom had abdominal pain and was admitted to Lions Gate Hospital. Initially, the doctor ran some tests and thought it was gallbladder or kidney stones. On Friday, July 13, Mom went in for surgery—it turned out to be stomach cancer that had either already grown deeply into the wall of her stomach or spread outside of it. Either way, it was too far advanced, and they just closed her back up. Mom woke up the following day, and I had a brief conversation with her, strangely, as if everything was normal. She passed away on Tuesday, July 17. I was 22, and my brother Amarith was 18.

We had no idea Mom might have been so ill, or that she wrote her last will and testament in that hospital bed. I definitely would have had a different conversation with my mom had I known more.

SOLARIE AND SOMA, 1986, MONTREAL

Author Reflection - Soma Keo
French Creek, BC, Canada

Dad passed away five years after Mom. We used the same funeral home, so they are together again in a beautiful memorial garden. I have stopped counting the years because sometimes it's easier not to. This writing process not only gave me a new perspective on my mom's life, but also led to the discovery of details regarding her childhood and previous life.

The gift of *My Mother's Story* has not only helped me heal by sharing with others, but has also given me the opportunity to preserve my family's story for future generations. It also reinforced my gratitude about being born in Canada rather than in Cambodia. My life would have been so different.

I wish I had tasted more of Mom's traditional Cambodian meals, something I did not start to appreciate until later in my adult years. But no one was really welcome in the kitchen while she was cooking, so I was never really taught how to cook. I wish she could taste the braised pork belly I have made a few times. I wish she could see her granddaughter growing up, attending Montessori school and learning French. I wish she could see the ways my brother and I have strengthened our relationship after we each grieved in our own ways.

Mom, I have finally come to understand everything you did for us. Even if we barely hugged or cuddled, I know how much you loved me and Amarith. My daughter, Keva, is four years old, and I hug and kiss her as much as I can—sometimes too much—and I know you would too. Her middle names are Stella Solarie.

I always tell Keva how much I love you and how I wish she could meet you. Occasionally, I cry out of nowhere and my daughter hugs me and says, "You will see your mom soon." She is right, you are everywhere. I hope that I looked at you the same way that Keva looks at me. Like Mitch Albom says, "When you look into your mother's eyes, you know that is the purest love you can find on this earth."

With every birthday, Mother's Day, or holiday celebration that goes by, I think of you, Mom. I just wish I could have told you in person, thank you for being so strict with me all those years, instilling those same traditional Cambodian values you also had growing up.

Although I was a young adult when you passed, and not a child or teen like some others in this anthology, I was still very young and our relationship had not yet progressed to one of friendship. Now, through writing your story, I can see you as a woman who might have become my friend.

Je t'aime Maman.

14 | Kelsey Weaver's Story of Nancy

Nancy Darlene Boyd was born in 1959 in the east end of Hamilton, Ontario, to Eleanor and Clifford, joining two siblings named Brian and Judy. They were raised in an extremely clean, safe environment that was juxtaposed with minimal rules and structure. The atmosphere was loving, and the children were well taken care of, however my uncle says at times the kids felt as though it was just five strangers living in the same house.

Nancy's mother, Eleanor, was born in Winnipeg into a traditional Ukrainian family of farmers who owned a general store. Nancy's father, Clifford, was born in Hamilton. The two met in 1940, fell in love, and got married a few months later.

They both came from chaotic, working-class families with eleven children each. Clifford was hardworking, friendly, and loving, whereas Eleanor appeared to have a tough nature. Underneath, she was very kind and would always be there for her family with a delicious home cooked meal. Unfortunately, Eleanor's parents didn't approve of her marriage to Clifford and disowned her until they were much older, when Eleanor was welcomed back to care for them.

As a child, Nancy was sensitive, creative, competitive, intelligent, and pretty well balanced. She loved Monopoly, playing outside, and reading books under her covers until late in the night. A high school friend says Nancy was the leader of their eccentric group of girlfriends. Apparently, even though they weren't cheerleaders, they would do things like dress in full cheer attire—pompom's and all—and cheer on the football team from the stands. Nancy would do anything for her girlfriends and she was the first one at their house to support them during a crisis.

After high school, Nancy was pressured to follow her mother's footsteps in nursing and entered college. Even though she had many gifts, nursing wasn't Nancy's true calling, and she left the program.

Nancy was introduced by friends to Steve a few years later at a party. Six months after that, they met by chance at a bar and started dating. Steve was kind, witty, and hardworking. At first Eleanor was suspicious of him, but Steve—my dad—says it wasn't long before she was "asking for his shirt size."

One day, on a date to teach Nancy how to drive, Steve asked her to make a left turn. Within seconds, they accidentally swerved onto someone's front lawn and Nancy and stopped the car in their wrought-iron fence. "Whoops" she said. "Well, that's okay, it needs more character; if anything, I was doing them a favour!" No one was hurt, the car was fine, and the fence only had a small dent. Steve laughed and rolled his eyes.

Nancy and Steve married on a crisp fall day in 1982. Nancy glowed in photographs that show her genuine smile in her beautiful lace dress. They rented a place in Hamilton and spent weekdays working and weekends partying with friends. She could often be found at a function, dressed to the nines, laughing her ass off with an Amaretto in hand. My dad says that when they went to the casino, she would smuggle in a bottle because it was her favourite and they did not sell it at the bar.

My mom had told me she never wanted to have kids, but that had all changed in 1990 when she was 31 and discovered she was pregnant. Nancy realized she now had a different purpose in life—to be the best mom she could be. She gave birth to a little girl they named Kelsey (that's me). Two years later, they had Michael—a sweet, but colicky baby with allergies who kept Mom busy. Mom and Dad provided a super clean, yet chaotic household, just like her mother's, but our home was filled with plenty of unconditional love, learning experiences, and quirky, fun moments.

Mom changed; instead of partying at the casino as she'd done in her youth, she now did things like throwing us the best birthday parties on the block. My fondest memories were of blasting our favourite songs and dancing in the living room—her smile glowing as I watched her flowing blonde bob do a dance of its own. "Kelsey, you have no rhythm," she would joke. "Here, watch what I do!" and she would show off her latest dance moves, using the coffee table as her stage. Then I'd snuggle with her, enveloped in her flowery scent—what my brother called "her inviting aroma"—and watch *Entertainment Tonight*. She was always there for Mike and me with a big hug, a kind smile, and chocolate milk.

In another fond memory, I remember one summer night, after the streetlights came on, my brother and I were outside playing with our friends. All of a sudden, we heard "woo-hoo" and saw our mom being pushed on a skateboard by one of her best friends and neighbours at the time. On Halloween, you would find the pair dressed in ridiculous costumes sitting in lawn chairs between the two houses giving out candy. If you watched long enough, you could hear them rate children's costumes following their own scale and laughing late into the night. After witnessing what the dynamic duo was up to, our neighbour's daughter and I would just look at each other, roll our eyes, and laugh. You wouldn't see any other moms behaving that way and we wouldn't have it any other way.

On my first day of grade one, I missed my bus home. Mom frantically raced to the school and when she saw me, hugged me tight with tears in her eyes. Then she held my hand as she marched into the principal's office and gave him a piece of her mind. I proudly witnessed her fierce 'momma bear' side in action.

Mom used her experience working in a bedding store and began staging the interiors of model homes. She started a successful interior design business called Beyond Windows in 1998. Mom was very talented at creating beautiful spaces, which was obvious when you visited any of the numerous homes she curated, especially ours. She was even featured in the newspaper several times for her stunning designs.

Mom's happy place was in her garden and she enjoyed teaching us everything she knew about horticulture. She would spend hours in the dirt, creating a beautiful serenity covered in flowers and plants of all sorts. The grass was as green as it could get, surrounded by gorgeous foliage. Hand-painted tulips created by her lined the bottom of the fence. Our neighbour fondly remembered Mom spraying her husband with the hose through the fence whenever she got the chance.

One of Mom's childhood friends told me how much she admired Nancy as a mother who loved her kids deeply. Mom provided us with many fun activities to do with her and worked hard to enroll us in a variety of extra-curricular activities. Every day after school, Mom would prepare a healthy snack and help us with our homework. If we asked for candy, Mom would always negotiate—we had to have a fruit or vegetable first—and then we would totally forget about the original treat.

Her friend also mentioned how obsessed Nancy was with brushing her teeth. Mom sure had beautiful white teeth! I remember how my mom dealt with Mike, who was a sensitive and smart kid but who hated brushing his teeth. Mom would give him a choice: easy way or hard way. Most of the time, he would choose wisely. However, when he didn't, Mom and I would pin him down and brush his teeth for him.

In 2002, when I was 11, Mom and Dad went through a separation and after trying their best to stay together, decided to get a divorce. My grandma, following in her parent's footsteps, disowned Mom for the next three years. This broke my mom's heart, and she vowed she would never do that to us, no matter what.

In 2003, Mom realized she couldn't cope with being a single parent and spent a short stint in Homewood Rehabilitation. Mike and I went to live with Dad and this was the first time I realized that my mom's mental health was not stable. I had always thought her weeks in bed were because she was sick, not depressed. While in the hospital, Mom sent several beautifully handwritten cards saying how proud she was of us and how much we were loved by her.

When she got out of the rehabilitation center, Mom rented an apartment nearby and continued her business and designing model homes. Mike and I, eleven and thirteen respectively, would stay with her on weekends. Mom would always make sure her place was with stocked with all our favourite foods and board games, especially Monopoly. She carefully kept track of every sporting event we had on her floral themed wall calendar and made sure she was in the front row of the stands to cheer us on. Every single day after school, Mom would phone to chat about our day and we would also excitedly plan our upcoming visits. Whether it was a craft fair, a new movie in theatres, an outdoor adventure, or a shopping trip to the mall, Mom always made sure we had something fun planned together to look forward to.

In 2005, Mom welcomed God into her life and even started going to church, where she would pray, rejoice, and even cry at times. She had always found friends anywhere, but the impact of these new church friends on her was huge. Mom also formed a stronger connection with her sister, Judy. Aunt Judy always adored my brother and became even closer with Mom when they could talk about God together. In May of 2007, Mom reunited with her mom, and they started to rebuild their relationship with each other. Grandma finally realized that they needed to be in each other's lives again.

Even though she was back on track, Mom still silently struggled with depression at times, but it didn't define who she truly was day to day. Her sister-in-law remembers vividly the day at a grocery store when Mom overheard two people fighting in the aisle next to her. Well, not having any of that, she marched over to their aisle and shouted, "STOP... Stop fighting. Life is too short for that, just love each other!" Anything she was passionate about, whether it was God, her kids, interior design, or apparently getting involved in stranger's lives, Mom embraced it wholeheartedly.

Over the years, Mom took several different medications to stabilize her mental health. In 2007, she was prescribed a new anti-depressant that we can only guess may have had adverse effects on her already fragile nervous system, including potentially affecting her thought processes. On the chilly, fall evening of October 25, 2007, my mom started a load of laundry, had some Amaretto, took her medication, relaxed into her hot bath, and never woke up. She was 47. We will never really know what happened that night or what was going through her mind.

Everyone was devastated to learn of her sudden death. Mom's funeral service was packed with grieving loved ones who remembered the incredible person she was. Aunt Judy sang a beautiful rendition of "Amazing Grace". On the car ride there, and only 17, I was persuaded to do a eulogy from the heart, which apparently didn't leave a dry eye in the place. After the service, Mom's 'people' stuck around a little longer, and that's when the real stories came out, and the party that truly celebrated her life officially started. We joyfully swapped hilarious and endearing stories of Mom until late into the night.

Mom was always in search of laughs and was notorious for finding humour in unexpected places. She was often misunderstood, but that didn't overshadow her generous nature, hardworking hands, and glimmering personality. At the end of the day, Mom loved fiercely, laughed like no one was watching, and would hug you like she was never going to let go.

NANCY, MIKE, AND KELSEY, 1993, HAMILTON, ONTARIO

Author Reflection - Kelsey Weaver
Coquitlam, BC, Canada

When I was approached to be included in this project, I was nervous, but a fire of curiosity was ignited inside me that shouted "yes!" without even knowing the details. Writing my mom's story often seemed like an impossible task, but what a good reason to feel her warm embrace in my soul again.

I have to admit, I was a bit naïve and struggled at times to surrender to the process. The amount of personal growth and understanding I gained about who I came from was worth every tear I shed. Indulging in deeper level conversations about her with friends and family was a blessing I didn't know I needed.

Along with the good memories and laughs I shared with everyone, came the pain that I had tucked away into a little jar; pain that I needed to feel and turn into something powerful. I needed to feel close to my beautiful mom again. To think it all started with a question… what did my mom teach me? All I could think at the time was, "don't burn your bridges," and above all else… don't die.

This opportunity brought me to new levels in the grieving process. I wrote a letter to my mom that I would like to share with you.

Dear Mom,

I miss you every day and often wonder what life would be like if you were here. Would you be living close to me? Would we still be dancing in the living room? Would we even get along? I think you would say "yes" to all those questions. Knowing you the way I do, I think you would still be filling everyone's lives with humour, love, compassion, and lots of quirky moments.

I have so many questions for you because I'm 31 now and I've had to grow up without you. With all my wonder, I know one thing for damn sure: even though life was hard for you—and even unbearable at times—you loved me unconditionally like no other. With that love and support you gave me for 17 years, I feel complete in an unexplainable way and that makes me feel like I can accomplish anything.

I'm sorry for the times I may have lashed out at you in my teenage 'know-it-all' years for things that aren't even important now. I wish we spent more time together in your last few years, so I could really appreciate all that you were.

There will always be a Nancy-shaped hole in the many hearts of those who loved you. I used to blame myself for your death, and I know Aunt Judy and your mom did too. However, writing your story has given me a whole new perspective. Although your illness won in the end, perhaps Mike and I gave you a good reason to press on longer than you would have otherwise.

Among the life lessons you shared with me, you taught me how to be brave in pursuit of being my authentic self in all that I do. To quote two lines in our favourite song by India Arie, "I learned to love myself unconditionally because I am a queen," and "My mama says a lady ain't what she wears, but what she knows."

I thank you for allowing me to share your beautiful, unique story and guiding me every step of the way. Even though you are not on earth anymore, you will always be alive in my memories, dreams, and most importantly, my heart.

15 | Mandy Gosling's Story of Jacqueline

It was late evening on April 16,1973, when Mum took her last breath in her own bed and died. She was 36 years old, and I was 9. Even though she had undergone a lumpectomy and radiotherapy, the breast cancer she had endured over the last year had finally taken its toll.

As her only child, I was taken in the dark of the night to my aunt's house, where I played unknowingly for three days until I was told by my great-aunt Mary that "Mummy has gone to heaven." There were no goodbyes.

It was Easter and Mum's funeral was arranged at the local church where she had married. It was full to capacity with all those that had known her; family and friends, the work colleagues from Provident where she had a part-time job, and the ladies from the Women's Institute. I was not there, but I was told the Easter egg that I had tucked away for her sat on top of her coffin amongst the flowers. A gift that would never be given.

Mum was born in High Wycombe, Buckinghamshire, England on May 12, 1936, during the time of the Wallis Simpson and King Edward VIII abdication scandal. Her parents named her Jacqueline Mary, and she had an older brother by 2 years and 4 months called Keith. It was said they were not particularly close growing up, but later, when they had their own children, they spent time together with their families. Mum's dad, Thomas Rutson, was a carpenter and had owned a building company since he was eighteen. Her mother, Queenie (her real name), had worked in the local laundry before she married Tom.

Mum's parents had both experienced early parental death: Tom's dad died when he was eighteen and Queenie's dad when she was five. One could imagine these early life losses influenced them personally and perhaps also later as parents. They lived in a modest bungalow, decked out with oak floors that Tom had fitted, and a large loft room for family functions and parties, as Queenie was the youngest of ten children. Mum's parents were quite different characters: Tom was a gentle, quiet man focused on providing for his family, and Queenie was steely and ran an efficient home. It was said that Queenie would often react to people who displeased her by giving them the silent treatment.

The family trademark of thick blonde curls did not escape Mum. As a child, she was always dressed immaculately in hand-knit cardigans and with ribbons in her hair. Everything was orderly in the bungalow, tasks undertaken with high standards, and there was a certain rigidity to everyday life. Washing was done on a Monday, ironing on a Tuesday, and each day the evening meal prepared after lunch. Each evening after dinner, the kitchen table was set for breakfast with a pristine tablecloth and place settings. I'm convinced Mum's early life was somewhat challenging with so many rules in place.

Mum was educated at the local convent, a private school deemed suitable by her parents, although not attended for religious reasons. I always knew that Mum was not interested in academics. It wasn't that she couldn't apply herself; she didn't want to!

Mum was close to her cousin Sheila, and they grew up like sisters. One Christmas, they conned both their parents to buy them bridesmaid dresses as a present to play dress up. I assume they were as thick as thieves in their plotting to get what they wanted. There are many pictures of Keith, Mum, and Sheila together as children. One is of Mum and Sheila as teenagers holidaying in Weymouth, wearing matching striped tops and berets. They went without their parents and stayed in a caravan, which I'm sure was a lot of fun. Mum's dad and her brother ran a local cycle speedway called Wycombe Wildcats, and every weekend Mum and Sheila would go and watch the teams race.

When Mum graduated school, she went to work at her dad's building company. I remember being told a story of her cutting glass by hand for the Hovis Bread Factory, which was an unusual task for a woman in the 1950s. She worked in the office and served customers in the building supplies store where both she and her brother worked. It was known that Mum was determined to reach her goal of owning her own home, and she worked hard to achieve this.

When Mum was seventeen, she met Ivan Scott at a local dance; he was later to become her husband. I always knew there was another man in her life at the time named Ivor, as it was such a similar name to Dad. There were letters in Mum's bedroom drawer between my parents mentioning Ivor and I'm still curious about what happened at that time in her life and how she chose who to marry.

Mum had quite a temper with Dad. Did he provoke that, or was it part of Mum's character? Six and two threes, perhaps. They must have felt something for each other though, as Mum and Dad married on June 4, 1960, at the Parish Church in High Wycombe, followed by a reception at the local British Legion, and a honeymoon on the island of Jersey at the Hotel L'Hermitage.

I learned what little I know about Mum's life in their early married years through her friend Sylvie, whom she met through their husbands' work. Sylvie told me that Mum and Dad's relationship seemed to have its difficulties. On July 28, 1963, Mum gave birth to me, and I was named Mandy Jayne. She suffered toxaemia in pregnancy, and I was delivered by emergency caesarean section. In those first few weeks of becoming a mum, she had to stay in hospital without me to recover.

In 1966, Mum found out that Dad was having an affair. It's unclear how she found out, but something happened at a dinner dance event at Dad's work. Apparently, Dad took Mum home and returned to his work event to be with another woman. Mum took a blade to her wrist and then called her dad, who drove her to the hospital in his pyjamas. Sylvie told me that Mum made Dad clean out his van with bleach and she even burned his clothes from that night!

The arguments continued at home and Mum made it clear to

those around her that it was difficult to trust Ivan. Mum became anxious after the affair and would try and keep the peace at home by making sure nothing upset Ivan. Perhaps this was to guarantee some security for herself and me, but I surmise it was a difficult experience. I would watch her change into fancier clothes every evening before his return home from work to be presentable, and she relied on medication to keep her stable.

Mum helped me with my schoolwork and she always found creative ways to teach me; like when she taught me fractions by drawing around pennies on paper and dividing them into segments while we sat in the garden. We spent time cooking together, and on Mondays we did the washing in the old tub.

Mum had a phobia of birds and every time she went to hang the washing on the line, she would panic and scream around the garden. She was a great cook and baked bread weekly. Measuring her ingredients to perfection, she baked the best cakes ever, especially for birthday parties. She was a protective mum and had a good sense of humour and would make my friends laugh. I recall her cheeky nature on a holiday in France when we were visiting a vineyard. She climbed out the back door of the coach and got back on again through the front door to get a second free bottle of wine!

At only 4 foot, 11½ inches, Mum playfully liked to say she was 5 feet. "That ½ inch makes all the difference," she would laugh. She had a magnetic smile that I still remember today. Her perfect, straight teeth were just like her dad's. Her dainty size 3 feet meant she could share her mules with me, and she would smile as I clip-clopped down the road. Her hair was short with curls, and she took a great deal of care in her appearance.

Her abundance of clothes was neatly sectioned out in her wardrobe. Day wear was typically fitted stirrup leggings and skinny turtlenecks with flat pumps. She had matching dresses and coats for more formal occasions, and there were a multitude of long dresses for parties. She taught herself to become a proficient seamstress and once made a 60s style woollen mustard shift dress that she teamed with white go-go boots—making sure I had a matching pair too!

Her favourite perfume was Tweed, which sat next to her makeup tray on the dressing table.

Mum had strong friendships with the women in our village, and for two summers these women fostered five children from a family whose mum had died. One child called Karen stayed with us and Mum became a mum to her, too. She showed Karen how to wash her hair and bought her clothes to take home after her stay with us.

When I was seven, Mum became pregnant. It would make sense this was an accident, as she was so unwell when I was born and had been told not to have any more children. I imagine it was a difficult decision to have a termination and tubal ligation, but I understand it was for her own safety that she could not go through with another pregnancy.

In 1971, Mum found a lump in her breast. Sylvie told me how frightened she was when she found it. At that time, my grandfather was dying of cancer and I can't remember anyone telling me, but I learned from somewhere that she put off her own medical investigations to focus on helping him and my grandmother. He died in 1972.

Mum wrote a letter to her Aunty Ivy (not her own mum) to help work out what she should do with her treatment. The letter revealed she only wanted to have the lump removed rather than a mastectomy because she was afraid it would upset Ivan if her body was not perfect. She would show me the scar on her breast when she sat in the bath, although she did not explain its significance. We will never know whether this choice had any impact on her chance of survival. I imagine this would have been a terribly difficult decision for Mum to make. In those days, reconstructive surgery was not an option, so she would fold face cloths into quarters and sew them into her bras to pad out what had been removed. Her orange bikini got the same treatment for our last family holiday together.

Mum underwent radiation therapy in Oxford, and I went with her to every appointment. I had certainly known too much of what was happening in my parents' life, but I was not told Mum was very sick and dying. She began to deteriorate and was given special permission to go on a holiday to Tunisia. Mum still smiled even though she was unwell, and her determination to enjoy life was still present. I later understood that her breast cancer had reached her liver. Although Mum's life was near its end, she never went into hospital and was able to stay at home.

I have felt some of Mum's sadness in her life story, but I can also see a mum who was determined, protective, fun, feisty, and an amazing cook. She taught me all of this alongside a deep love of family and children. All of this continues through me and to her two grandchildren.

JACQUELINE AND MANDY, 1973, TUNISIA

Author Reflection - Mandy Gosling

High Wycombe, Buckinghamshire, England

I wasn't sure what to expect when writing my mother's story. Forty-eight years after Mum's death, I had left who she was far behind in my memory. When I wrote my first draft, I used the word Mother instead of Mum. I think this was an unconscious effort to keep the next layer of pain at a distance and, of course, this ultimately kept me away from my connection to her. Even though I've been in therapy, and am a therapist myself, I've learned over the years that processing childhood bereavement is a lifetime's work.

I took the plunge and rewrote from the first person to really immerse myself, which brought the connection to my mum that much closer. I began to realize there was no escape from facing another layer of painful feelings, even if not as intense as some of the previous times. Over the years, I've come to appreciate this is my life's journey, to understand more of what happened to me as a child, and revisit what I could not do then. Through this, I have healed more than I ever imagined possible, and this is what allows me to live more of my own life.

There were things in Mum's story that I knew, but through this process there are things that I *really know* now—a felt sense of her lived experience. Through writing, it has allowed me to viscerally connect with the woman she was. I found a mum who had enough feist to keep her going and a woman smart enough to work out what to do. She was protective of me, and I have strongly felt that I really was her world. The values she held around family, food, and love are as strong today through me as they were with her. These are the gifts she gave to me.

After Mum died, she was never talked about. As a child, I would often try on her clothes to feel close to her. I wanted to write her story to honour her and to pass onto my own children so they could know her too. I had mixed feelings throughout, moments of laughter at some of her antics and quirks, and sadness at times when I felt her inability to perhaps live as she wanted to. Her life was different to mine, but I could see a normal life of ups and downs with family and relationship struggles.

Writing Mum's story has given me a deeper sense of gratitude for my own life. I've lived an interesting life with courage and even some of the same struggles as Mum. I've also had the chance to make different decisions, and in some cases, change the family patterns. This opportunity to freely choose means I can be my own woman. *My Mother's Story* has given me another layer of healing. Of course, I know there will be more layers—there are always more layers—and they come generally when I'm least expecting it!

16 | Colleen Rhodes' Story of Jean

The last time I saw my mom alive, she was lying in a hospital bed, waiting for my arrival. It was September 1, 1986. She had asked me to come and wash her hair since it hadn't been washed in over a week. I could tell when her big, brown eyes caught sight of me that she was happy to see me. She seemed to be in much better shape than the last time I visited. When she got up out of bed and walked to the bathroom with her IV stack in tow, the blue hospital gown gaped open at the back, revealing her buttocks, stained with dried blood.

Taken aback, but not inquiring, I set about to get her thin, straight, black hair shampooed and conditioned. Once back in bed, she applied some makeup to help her feel normal again. She looked good, she looked healthier, but I didn't know what was wrong with her. I didn't ask, she didn't tell, and I wouldn't find out for 13 more years. She left this world the next day.

Jean Anne Rock was born on November 19, 1942, to Cecil Edward Rock and Frances Mahoney. She was the only child they would have, for reasons I do not know. She made up for the lack of siblings with aunts, uncles, and cousins, some of whom lived with them in their house at 36 Wallace Ave, near Dufferin and Bloor Street in Toronto. Her favourite, Uncle Jim, was never short of pranks to play on her there, including once nailing her slippers to the floor, so she fell flat on her face when she got up in the morning.

One of the few things I know about my mother's childhood was that she went to Dufferin Street Presbyterian Church because I have the Bible she received for Sunday School attendance when she was 16. Four years later, in the summer of 1962, at the tender age of 20, she lost her father to heart failure.

A few months after her father's death, Mom went on a blind date set up by mutual friends. His name was Donald John Rhodes. As fate would have it, Jean turned out to be the love of his life. Mom and Dad got engaged a year later and married a year after that on November 7, 1964, followed by a honeymoon in Florida. Souvenirs brought home from that trip (like seashells and postcards) remained in the cedar chest for the rest of her life—taken out and played with every so often by me and my sister.

Mom and Dad moved into their first house, at 15 Stonehenge Crescent, in the Toronto suburb of Scarborough in 1968. During that time, Mom's mom (Grandma Fran) married a man named Arthur Heywood and moved to Arbor Road in Mississauga, Ontario. Arthur became "Art" to Jean and eventually "Grandad" to me and my sister.

Mom gave birth to my sister, Heather Elane, on August 1, 1968. When Heather was barely a year old, my parents took her camping in their tent trailer to the east coast of Canada. It was there, in Baddock, Nova Scotia, during the Summer of 1969, that Mom conceived me. On April 28, 1970, I was born—Colleen Andrea.

Grandma Fran passed down to my mom the superstition that it was lucky to have the initials of your name spell a word. Even after marriage, Mom remained a JAR, and my sister and I were a HER and a CAR, respectively.

After my sister and I were born, Mom decided she would quit work to stay home and raise us. A neighbour told me that our mother loved us so dearly that "the sun rose and set" around us. I didn't need to be told that, though; she showered us with love and affection.

We spent every Sunday at Grandma Fran and Grandad's house and most holidays with Mom's extended family of aunts and uncles who lived just down the road. One day in 1977, Dad told us that Mom wasn't feeling well and was going to stay in bed that day. We found out later that it was because her mother had died from lung cancer. After that, Grandad would spend every Sunday at our house smoking cigars, playing the organ, and having dinner with us.

As my sister and I got older, Mom felt the need to occupy herself with more than just cooking and cleaning. She started working part-time at Central Ceramics and discovered a love for painting, staining, and airbrushing pottery. Eventually, she converted the basement into a ceramics studio, complete with kiln for firing greenware. Mom painted Christmas trees with shiny green glaze, adding puffy snow and sparkles to the branches and glued in coloured plastic Christmas lights. She painted pitchers and bowls with pretty decals and made cookie jars, and tons of large garden gnomes.

I was most fascinated by the boob and penis mugs that lined her metal shelves in various stages of finish. She airbrushed them with lifelike accuracy and sold them to my father's co-workers at Canadian Tire as well as to The Pink Shoppe—a commissioned craft store in Nestleton, Ontario. Neighbours on Stonehenge and Bailey Crescent came over for ceramics lessons, including the single middle-aged man who lived next door to us with his parents. We always teased Mom that he had a crush on her.

I don't really know Mom's whole story or what happened next, but I do know lots of little things. Here is some of what I do know for sure:

- She struggled with her weight for most of her adult life, but that's what made her hugs extra special and all-enveloping. She was firm when necessary, but super soft when you needed it most. She was the type of woman that you wanted as much of the soft side as you could get. She raised us to be kind and considerate and expected nothing less from those we hung out with.

- Mom loved to play guitar and sing John Denver songs with her beautiful voice. She danced with us in the living room to disco songs in the 70s, played cribbage on the front porch during thunderstorms, and did puzzles on the teak dining room table for hours, listening to Abba.

- She wore wigs and hairpieces to fluff up her flat hair, gave Eskimo kisses, and always said "I love you" at bedtime.

- She gave us Pepto Bismol when we were sick, even though it made me toss my pink cookies every time.

- Mom hid the Christmas presents from Santa in the back room, thinking no one would look there or discover that Santa was not real.
- She said sugar instead of sh*t until we were old enough to say it ourselves. She put Saccharin in her tea instead of sugar until it was banned in 1981.
- Mom didn't like to cook because she wasn't very good at it. Either that or she wasn't very good at cooking because she didn't like it. I'm not really sure which one is true, but I do know that she passed that gene along to me.
- She gave my sister and I home haircuts one summer and said we couldn't get our ears pierced until we were 16, but eventually gave in years earlier.
- Mom volunteered with the neighbourhood baseball league that my sister and I played in, organizing tournaments and working at the snack table.
- She sent me and my sister to our friend's cottage every year with a watermelon.
- Mom watched her favourite shows on a TV that was perched on the dryer in the basement. She sat in a green tweed chair and would brush my hair while I sat on the floor in front of her.
- When she wasn't brushing my hair, Mom was grabbing a knitting needle from the magazine rack next to her chair to scratch her ears.
- Mom had a pretty face, a beautiful smile, and the most infectious laughter. Pictures never did her any justice, as most photos exhibit a crooked smile with a look of "just take the picture already." Her good nature, terrific sense of humour, and sunny disposition didn't always shine through in photographs, but you definitely felt it just being around her.
- Mom was the type of woman who, even in her secret terminal illness, would have crawled her way out of the hospital to the wedding of a dear friend.

Had I known she was dying, I would have stayed by her bedside that last day. A woman who put everyone else's needs in front of her own should not have to die alone, and she succumbed in the middle of the night.

My mother's life, looking back, might not appear remarkable, but she was a remarkable woman, if not just for her kind and gentle nature. She would never have chosen to leave us, but the universe had other plans for her, and needed her light to shine somewhere else.

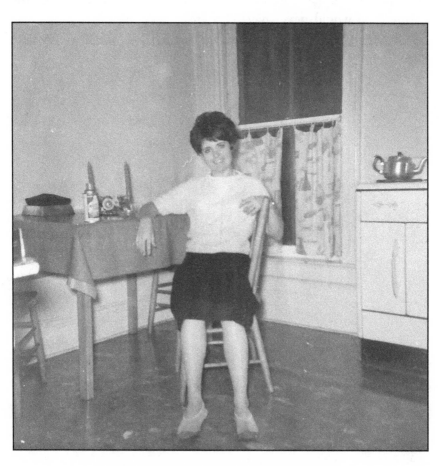

JEAN, 1964/65, WALLACE AVE KITCHEN

Author Reflection - Colleen Rhodes
Burnaby, BC, Canada

As I write this reflection, I am approaching the 35th anniversary of my mother's death. My 16-year-old self had no idea what impact that event would have on every aspect of my life. My adult self can't believe how it still manages to intricately weave its way into how I react to many situations.

Writing my mother's story was a challenge for me in many ways, starting with how very little I knew about my mother. I could write about how fiercely I loved her, but where did she go to school? What was her first job? Did she marry her first love? What were her hopes and dreams? I didn't know the answers to any of these questions, and it made me feel guilty and selfish to consider that I never took the time to find out much about Mom.

Secondly, there are not a lot of people still alive to ask about her. I connected with a few family members and friends who knew Mom well, but most of what I was able to retrieve was that she was a lovely and kind woman. I knew that already. I lived it and loved her for it.

Third, I have some kind of memory block. There is a wall in my brain, with a few bricks missing here and there. I can peer in and see some memories, but others are trapped in the recesses. I'm not sure if they'll ever be released. Having met other women who lost their mothers in infancy or childhood, I thought I was one of the 'lucky' ones because I didn't lose my mom until I was a teenager. I felt I should have a memory advantage over others who experienced early loss, but I quickly realized that wasn't the case.

Lastly, in writing this story, I always knew that I could not be completely open about the circumstances surrounding Mom's death. She did not want anyone to know the truth about her disease, and I wanted to honour that. This was the biggest challenge for me because my writing has always come from an honest place in my heart.

Ultimately, these challenges set me on a path of discovery and healing. I reconnected with people from my past whom I otherwise may not have. I dug up information that I never knew before. As I learned little tidbits about Mom, I learned about myself, became more self-aware and conscious of our similarities, and made positive lifestyle changes because of it.

I was so used to answering the tragic questions about how and when Mom died, it makes sense that it was uncomfortable to talk about. Writing about her as a woman; who she was, what she did, and thinking about her from a different point of view, has been so cathartic. I am no longer haunted during the week leading up to the anniversary of Mom's death. I don't always need to be upset about the sad parts, and I can celebrate the happy ones too.

17 | Jennifer Burgie's Story of Kimberley

"Jennifer... Jennifer, wake up, sweety!"

The sun had barely risen high enough to shine through the covered windows when I opened my eyes. Kneeling next to the bed, my mom was smiling at me, the pale light casting a faint glow around her silhouette, as though she were an angel. Her hair fell in her face as she bent over me, but I could still see the big smile on her face, and the sparkle in her eye. For my mom to be awake before me was very curious, so I scurried from under the covers to follow her outside.

"Shhh, quietly," Mom said as she knelt and coaxed me to sit against her legs in front of her. That's when I saw it; a gorgeous, giant dragonfly perched on one of the bands of an old, frayed, green and white lawn chair.

"He's eating a bee," she whispered. "That's why he doesn't fly away." As she spoke, she very lightly ran her finger down the impossibly black, yet glinted green back of the insect.

"Gently," she said, as she guided my hand forward and curled my other fingers under so that only my index stuck out. She looked at me and smiled the smile I'd seen a thousand times before, but each time felt like the first. I could feel her love shining through that smile, the way her head tilted slightly to the side, and that sparkle that no one could resist.

To my child-aged brain, I thought life was perfect. My mom was the most fun person in the world, but as I grew up, I would come to understand that she was a very haunted woman with a very good mask.

Kimberley Louise Burgie was born on October 18, 1960, at Grace Hospital in Toronto, the middle child of three girls. Her parents were Helen Miranda, the middle child of seven, and Leo Burgie, one of thirteen children. They came from very different upbringings. Both from Metis heritage, Leo's family was loving and close, the product of parents who were star-crossed lovers, climbing mountains to be together. Helen's family, however, always lived in fear of their alcoholic father. Helen couldn't wait to get away from her family, so when she met Leo at a roller-skating disco one night, she dove into that relationship. Within a short time, they were married in 1953, and their first daughter was born in 1954.

Helen worked for a bigshot defence lawyer in Toronto, and she loved to tell stories of taking calls from convicted criminals. When her firstborn, Sandra, came around, she took an extended leave from work to raise her daughter. Helen found it hard to be away from work for so long, so when Mom was born, she arranged to have her live with an Aunt (Tee Tee) from Monday to Friday until Mom was five. Perhaps seeing how this affected my mom, Helen decided again to stay home when Mom's sister Vicki was born in 1965. Perhaps it was due to this set of circumstances that Mom would grow up to feel unloved and unwanted by her family, exhibiting signs of depression and anxiety at an early age.

As a young adult, Mom obsessed with her appearance. She would spend hours doing her hair and makeup. Because of this passion, and being a high school dropout, she decided to go to hairdressing school. When this didn't satisfy her, she got a job at Fairweather's as a sales associate. She loved working there, especially for the store discount on clothes and accessories. She would buy herself fancy outfits for going out with her friends. She did so frequently, mostly to bars where she would receive a lot of attention from men. She relished this attention and was promiscuous, always choosing men who treated her poorly. Included in these men was Howard Shannon, who would end up being my biological father.

I was born on August 14, 1981, when my mother was 21. I immediately became the light of my mother's life. She was so proud of me and would take me anywhere she could to show me off, so much so that I earned the nickname Little Kimmy. When Howard learned of Mom's pregnancy, he immediately started to pull away from her. After I was born, she took me to meet him once, but that would be the first, last, and only time I saw him in person.

Mom spoiled me, taking me everywhere and buying me My Little Pony dolls for my collection. She would throw me birthday parties and hire my aunt to play a clown and buy crazy, intricate Rainbow Bright cakes. As I look back on this now, I can see that my mom worked hard to give me the childhood that she missed out on.

When she realized she needed more money and had to stop spending so much on fashion, she reluctantly gave up the retail job for an office job in an insurance firm. That's where she met Rob. Mom fell for Rob right away, telling her sisters how she had a crush on this guy at work. The intimate part of their relationship started with Mom offering to dye Rob's hair. Rob also had a part-time job at a bar downtown, and my mom would go and hang out with him while he worked. They quickly fell in love, and before I knew it, the three of us lived in an apartment down the street from my grandparents' house.

Mom was very protective; some might even say paranoid. We lived on a residential street, where 95% of the traffic was local, but I was not allowed to cross the street alone to go to my friend's house. If I wanted to walk to visit my grandparents, Mom would watch from our apartment, and my grandpa would watch from his house until I was with him.

Mom found out around this time that she was pregnant, and she decided that the family would move to London, Ontario, because Toronto was not a safe place to raise a family. She had an aunt and uncle who lived in London, and they found us a townhouse in their complex. Robert Andrew was born on July 12, 1988, and we moved to London in October.

Rob and my mom married in May of 1989, when Mom was seven months pregnant with her third child. Thomas Jordan was born on July 12, 1989, and together we were a happy and loving family. To me, my mom looked like a confident woman who loved her children, but I learned later in life that she was depressed. She cried to her sisters that she felt like she was a bad mom, and that she was always sad. They urged her to try and do new things to feel more like herself again, so, she hired a babysitter, and went back to work. Finally, having something other than being a mom seemed to help my mom's mental health, and she was able to feel more satisfied when she was at home. After finding a job, she decided that helping others would also make her feel better, so she started donating blood to the Red Cross.

A few weeks later, Mom received a letter in the mail from the Red Cross, informing her of an irregularity in her blood, and that she should go and see a doctor. Although she had concerns about the letter, she did not expect to get the results that came in. The irregularity they found was AIDS.

She told Rob, as he would have to get tested as well. His results came back HIV+, which was not good but not quite as dire as Mom's diagnosis. Rob, being a bi-sexual man, immediately assumed he was the cause, but Mom wouldn't hear it. She had had a blood transfusion years earlier, and so she insisted there was no way to tell; and even if there was, she wouldn't want to know. She didn't ever want there to be the possibility of resentment, since the next chapter of their journey would already be frightening enough.

Fearing the worst, they got all three children tested. My parents were absolutely devastated when it came back that both sons were also positive; the youngest, Tom, with HIV, and sadly, the older of the two, Robby, with AIDS. The doctor was direct and honest and told Mom that she and Robby only had two years to live. Right away, my mother lost her will to live. It was almost like she resolved that she was going to die and gave up. She did hold some Christian faith, and once told Rob that she wanted to be in heaven before any of her children so that they didn't have to be alone.

The medications for HIV/AIDS in the early 90s were not highly effective, and the mortality rate was high. Mom didn't care about the medication's implications on her—all she wanted was the best for her children. I could see the pain in her eyes as she had to watch her sons take a vile liquid treatment that made them feel awful.

Both Mom and Rob were fired from their jobs due to their diagnosis in 1990. My mother realized how little was known about HIV/AIDS at that time and decided that her final years would be spent helping educate the public on what the disease was, and to try to stop the spread of shame and stigma that is still prevalent today. She travelled to schools and communities in London and the neighbouring counties in Ontario from 1991-92 to inform children and adults about how HIV was spread and how people with HIV and AIDS were not to be feared.

This work seemed to energize her. She had a purpose, and she felt the importance of that work. Due to Mom's efforts, our family earned a celebrity status of sorts, as she would get us booked on local broadcast talk shows and was featured in newspaper articles.

All the while, her body was slowly succumbing to the disease. Almost weekly, she would appear more fragile, lose more weight, and get weaker. By the end of 1992, she was pretty much bound to the couch with an IV, waking from time to time until she got up and went to bed. That is, when she wasn't in the hospital. Hospital stays grew longer and became more frequent. I visited her so much in the hospital that I was not surprised to visit her there. Because of this, I didn't realize that one visit on May 15, 1993, would be the last time that I would see my mother.

KIMBERLEY AND JENNIFER, 1981, TORONTO, ONTARIO

Author Reflection - Jennifer Burgie

Vancouver, BC, Canada

I was thrilled when I was invited to submit a piece in the *My Mother's Story* anthology. There was a lot about my mother that was a mystery to me, coming from a family that rarely speaks about the difficult things, and I was afraid I would come up short. My mother's sisters are the only living family I could ask, and while they both worried how I'd react, they agreed to finally share the truth with me.

I knew our family had secrets, from the fact that my grandmother refused to mention her father, to a lifetime of observing that everyone ignored issues and avoided conflict. A lot of what I learned was indeed hard to hear, but in the end, I feel more connected to my family after learning all the hardships many of them had to endure. I can understand why no one wants to remember, let alone speak, of these unimaginable events.

I knew the story of my mother after her diagnosis; I was around for all of that. It was her early years that rattled me. I had no idea of her struggles back then, and it broke my heart to learn how troubled she had been. Growing up in my grandmother's house with her, before our move to London, I only remember how she was a joyful mom. I felt a deeper connection with her after learning the truth, as I struggled with the same insecurities, masks, and pain. I have read about childhood trauma, and I was familiar with the theory of it being passed down intergenerationally. When I look at the emotional turmoil my mom and grandmother both endured as well, I can't help but find truth to that idea.

After the research, the piece was incredibly emotional to write. I struggled with a few obstacles during the writing process, and sometimes I found I lacked the emotional energy it took. Remembering those last years with my mom was painful because I hold so much shame over not realizing how dire things were. I wish I had been more perceptive and sentimental then, so that I would have known the importance of the last words we exchanged.

Although it's been nearly 30 years since her passing, I still feel that loss greatly. I don't for one minute regret writing her story, though. What I have learned about my mom and how I see her in a more rounded way is a gift, a beautiful one, and one I will always be grateful for.

18 | Shenan Marie Smith's Story of Melody

Early every morning, while I got ready for school, Mom hustled about. She packed my lunch, made sure my school bag and I were ready, and managed to get herself prepared for the long drive to nursing school. Once loaded into the car, she would drive the half mile down our driveway and wait at the bottom of the hill until the bus arrived. She'd give me a hug and a kiss and tell me she loved me. On the morning of September 8, 1992, we argued. What about, I honestly have no recollection. But as I left the car, we didn't say goodbye. We didn't say I love you. Little did I know that this would be the last time I would see her alive. And for years, I'd regret our fight, and wish I'd said I love you.

This is my mother's story, *written from her perspective*, as I've imagined it.

I was a natural birth, born to June and Robert Bailey in Springfield, Massachusetts on Friday, August 1, 1958, at 4:43pm. My mother was 31 years old, and my father was 35. At the time I was born, my older sister and brother, Roxanne ("Roxie") and Robert ("Bob"), were eleven and five. Mom wanted to name me Priscilla, but Roxie suggested Melody. After some discussion, the name stuck. Mom liked the name Lynn, so that was chosen as my middle name.

I was the third child born into a family who didn't know they wanted me until I was born. Times were hard and money was tight. I often joked with my mother that I wasn't wanted. I knew differently, though, as evidenced by the love my family showed me, even in the roughest of times.

Dad was in the Air Force, serving as an airplane mechanic. We moved often because he was transferred about every three years.

From Springfield, we went to Barksdale Air Force Base in Bossier Parish, Louisiana. Then we were off to Holland Patent in Rome, New York, and when I was about six or seven, we moved to Puerto Rico. The base was on the upper northwest tip of the island, and we lived in a concrete home with banana trees in the small backyard on Lighthouse Drive. On hot summer days, Mom would hose the house down inside and out to keep it cool.

I loved Puerto Rico. I went to class with the other children that lived on the base, and after school I was free to explore the surrounding grounds. I rode my bike everywhere, spent time at the pool near the beach, and played school with the neighbourhood children. I was always the teacher. When children weren't around or after they left because I was too bossy, I'd substitute my stuffed animals for students. A neighbour owned a stable near the beach, and I started to help take care of the horses there, learning how to groom, muck stalls, and best of all, ride! We also got our first dogs in Puerto Rico—first Sheba, a black shepherd/malamute mix, then Eric, a German Shepherd. Mom let me be Eric's trainer. I gained my independence in Puerto Rico, a trait I maintained throughout my life.

When I was ten, Dad was worried he'd be sent to Vietnam, so he decided to retire from the Air Force and move us somewhere he'd always liked the idea of living—Lancaster, Ohio. Life was different there. The kids made fun of me because my bright blonde hair and tanned skin were different. Ohio's rainy, gloomy days didn't give them my sun-kissed glow. I wasn't able to roam the neighbourhood like I used to in Puerto Rico. Since we weren't on a government base anymore, Mom said it wasn't safe, so I found new hobbies like twirling the baton, and my companion, Eric, was still with us.

When I was in high school, Mom and Dad bought a larger house in Reynoldsburg. Here, during my sophomore year, I met Mark. I'd seen him around, but we'd never spoken. One night, I had a dream he would ask me out. The very next day, Mark approached me in study hall. As he started to ask me out, I could feel my mouth drop. I couldn't believe I'd had an actual premonition! Mark was a tall, dark, handsome, compassionate go-getter. I felt like a lucky girl.

After dating for a few years, Mark and I decided—against our parents' wishes—to move in together. We chose an apartment near The Ohio State University. We both started making decent money; Mark as an apprentice carpenter and me as a dental hygienist. We decided to tie the knot on April 28, 1978, at the small, non-denominational chapel at Rickenbacker Air Force Base. I made my own dress, and Roxie did my hair and makeup. I wasn't very traditional, so I chose a light blue fabric with off-white lace for the trim. It was mainly family who attended our wedding and reception, but it was a beautiful day. At age 20, I was now Mrs. Melody Wentworth.

As Mark's career blossomed, we moved to Virginia for his new role building houses. We found a little house in Fairfax and settled in. Mark worked on fixing up the inside of the house. Our new family of two expanded to four as we welcomed Cybil and Rhea—two Terrier-mix sisters. We lost Rhea soon after, but Cybil thrived for many years to come. I loved having dogs of my own.

I soon learned I was pregnant; I was terrified, but excited at the same time. Those nine months seemed to last forever. Mark wanted to take pictures, but I never felt in the mood. I never really liked having my picture taken.

On a Sunday evening, I went into labour. Mark rushed me to the hospital. Several hours later, our girl still wasn't making her entrance. The doctor recommended a caesarean. Being just the two of us, the rest of our family still in Ohio, we prepared ourselves and decided to trust the doctor. The surgery lasted for hours. While Mark waited, he got in touch with Mom. I think he was in shock because he could only murmur that I was in surgery.

I don't recall all of the birth. Mark says he almost lost both of us. Once awake, I was greeted by my healthy, beautiful daughter. She was born at 11:42 pm on Monday, May 5, 1980, weighing nine pounds, seven ounces. As I held her for the first time, I was in awe. I'd never loved anyone like this. We decided to name her Shenan Marie, after our love of the Blue Ridge Mountains, particularly

Shenandoah Park. Mark became the primary provider; I stayed home to take care of Shenan. Early on, we took her swimming and on walks with Cybil through the Shenandoah and Blue Ridge Mountains.

As in childhood, I moved frequently in adulthood. When the 1980s recession began, and work dried up in Virginia, Mark and I moved back to Ohio. His Dad owned a duplex, so we moved into one side, while Mark's brother Pat and his wife, Sally, lived on the other. Mark took several consecutive contractor positions with different local home builders, and I continued to stay home with Shenan. Our family expanded as we adopted a black Labrador mix, Cole, and a calico kitten, Cleo.

We found a small house to rent in Pickerington, a growing suburb near both our parents. Shenan began kindergarten in a good school district, and I began volunteering at the horse barn across the street. I hadn't been around horses since Puerto Rico, and this was something I wanted to share with Shenan. Enter Brodie, a tall, dark brown Tennessee Walker who had the gentlest personality. He eventually became ours, and the three of us spent countless hours with him. In his later years, I'd find Shenan curled up with him in the field when he was taking a nap.

Mark's experience gave him the confidence to start his own business building houses. I handled the bookkeeping, graphic design, and marketing. As his company grew, we were able to buy our first house, an old, burned-out farmhouse sitting on five acres in the outskirts of Pickerington. We fixed it up to perfection. Mark built a new barn and we moved Bodie in, along with our new horse Appie, a sweet, red roan Appaloosa with a cantankerous side.

After a few years, we found an opportunity to buy a much larger plot of farmland down the street. After selling the farmhouse, we soon found ourselves sleeping in the back of the pickup truck under the roof of the new barn Mark built on the property. It was tough, but we made it work. Mark converted the front of the barn into a house. Our goal was to build a larger house later but, unfortunately, those plans never came to fruition. Mark's business failed, and he was forced to take a job driving a truck cross-country. The money was good, but he wasn't home much.

Mark built an additional barn on the property that was big enough for not only Bodie and Appie, but a new horse, a Thoroughbred named Misty. And, knowing I wanted to train a yearling, I found Rusty-Nail, a tall, beautiful, rust-coloured Tennessee Walker with a grey muzzle. When Shenan was in third grade, I rode him down to her school for a show and tell demonstration, complete with a homemade instruction booklet on horse handling. We were a hit.

Wanting to give Shenan the opportunity to train an animal herself, we adopted Max, a grey Doberman Pinscher, when she was in fourth grade. I surprised her by getting an early dismissal and bringing Max into Shenan's class to meet her. To help Shenan learn how to train Max properly, I began a 4-H club for her and some of her close friends. Shenan helped me name the group, K-9 Krazy, and we started attending parades and 4-H dog shows.

With Shenan getting older, and Mark on the road, I started to think about how I could contribute more to our household and Shenan's future. I decided to look into nursing and found an expedited Registered Nursing program at Central Ohio Technical College that would only take two years to complete. I took classes while Shenan was in school, which allowed me to be there for her when she was home. I studied after dinner, which was hard on Shenan, but I think she understood this would help us in the long run.

As I progressed through the program, I eagerly anticipated my graduation. By September 1992, I'd be done. Shenan was twelve, in junior high, and I had just turned thirty-four. On September 8, I had roughly two weeks until graduation. That morning, I drove to the bottom of the driveway and waited with Shenan for her bus. At 6:50 am, she was on her way. I popped a pre-recorded tape I'd made to help me study into the cassette player and headed down the back roads toward campus.

It was a sunny day; the temperature in the mid-70s. I'd made this hour drive down the winding two-lane roads to the Mount Vernon campus many times before.

About mid-way through, as I approached some hilly terrain in an area with a double yellow line, suddenly a truck was coming towards me in my lane. There wasn't any time or anywhere to go. I was going about 60 mph, and he was likely going faster.

It was around 7:10 am when we hit head on. According to my death certificate, the paramedics estimated I only survived about another five minutes. In those minutes, I thought about my beautiful daughter. I hoped she knew how much I loved her, and that Mark would be there for her.

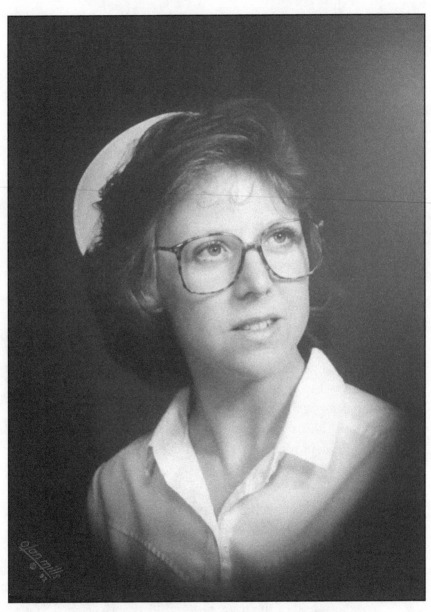

MELODY, 1992, OLAN MILLS STUDIO, OHIO

Author Reflection - Shenan Smith

Columbus, Ohio, USA

My mom was my everything. After she died, and for many years to come, the world just didn't seem as bright without her. It's taken me years since her passing to properly grieve her, and writing this piece has been one of my most healing experiences. Not only have I learned new facts about my mom's childhood, but her essence has come back to me, along with many memories. Through this writing, I've remembered:

- She read to me every night, sewed us matching outfits, and helped me with my homework.
- She was very organized—everything had its place in our home.
- She knew what she wanted out of life and how to plan for the future.
- She had gorgeous blue-hazel eyes that usually appeared light blue, but sometimes took on a green tint.
- She'd normally be found in a pair of jeans and a t-shirt or button-down flannel, and hardly ever wore makeup. Saturdays, when we attended church, were the one exception—she'd put on a simple but elegant dress paired with sandals or boots, apply a light coat of foundation, some mascara, a tinted lip gloss, and add the tiniest hint of White Shoulders perfume to her neck and wrists.
- When she'd work with the horses or in the yard, she always wore a hand-crocheted headband.
- She loved roller and ice skating and taught me how to do both as she skated backwards, always holding my hands and catching me if I'd fall.
- Growing up in the 70s, Mom loved listening to the most popular music of the time. She and Dad both learned to play guitar, and she sang to me quite often, Shenandoah being the most frequent lullaby.

I was hungry for information and details. Talking to my aunt and uncles not only gave me the answers I sought, but helped me learn their perspective of life when they were all young. Through this experience, I learned the importance of writing about my memories for myself and not letting others' memories or beliefs alter my view. Memories shift, fade, and can become distorted over time, but holding true to my own beliefs is what matters most.

I'd heard stories from everyone telling me how she died, but getting my mom's death certificate and seeing the words on paper, while hard, helped me a lot. Learning about the true nature of her death brought me face to face with imagining how she spent the last few minutes on this earth. Once I knew that, I was able to piece together a lot and process my feelings completely.

This year will mark 30 years since Mom passed. She's been gone now for almost three-quarters of my life, and as time passes the fraction that I had her in my life will continue to dwindle. I'm forever grateful to have been a part of this writing experience, which has allowed me to put some of the facts about her into writing. I'll cherish this, as I will her, always.

19 | Amanda McNally's Story of Penny

On a winter evening in Suffolk, England, in February of 1946, my mother, Penelope Ann ("Penny") Hack, made her entrance into the world. As the family lore goes, she was born in the seventh month of her mother's pregnancy, weighing just three pounds two ounces, and slid down her mother's pyjama leg onto the kitchen floor just as she returned from the outhouse. There was no heat in the house, so Nanna scooped her up, wrapped her in towels, and popped Penny into the oven to be kept warm with the heat from the pilot light until the local visiting nurse arrived the following morning.

Although she had a dramatic and shaky start, Mom grew stronger each day. After a few months, Nanna and Mom were able to board a ship with other war brides and head to Halifax, Nova Scotia. From there, they travelled to Montreal, Quebec, to reunite with her father, Robert. Robert, known as "Bob" or "Bobby" to all, including his grandchildren, was a Canadian soldier who had returned to Canada following World War II. Nanna had been unable to travel back to Canada to join Bob due to her pregnancy, so she had remained in Suffolk with family until Mom was born.

Mom developed a severe intestinal infection and had to be hospitalized when she was six months old. At one point, her condition had worsened to a life-or-death situation, and Nanna and Bob were told to prepare for the worst. Fortunately, Mom fought her way back to health and began to thrive. As a result of being a preemie, Mom had quite a small head but very large ears as a child. Mom's grandmother, Elsie, used to say that she looked like a taxicab coming down the street with its doors open. Thankfully, she grew into her ears by the time she started school.

Mom was the eldest of six: three sisters and two brothers—Lynda,

Robin, Robert ("Bobby"), Laurel, and Nicholas ("Nick"). From the beginning, Mom assumed a responsible, nurturing role over her younger siblings. My grandfather was in the Royal Canadian Air Force (RCAF) and had his own insurance business in town, so he was often out of the house. Mom was there as Nanna's right hand, and Nanna came to really rely on her.

She was both the babysitter and her mother's helper. She was also Nanna's assistant with baking, cooking, cleaning, and other chores as needed. Over the years, Mom developed different relationships with each of her siblings, but she was always the big sister. They were close, spending a lot of time together. However, they were not immune from the usual sibling drama. There was unrest when it was discovered that Mom could stay up later, that certain rules didn't apply to her as the eldest, and there was the friction of her always being left in charge.

Growing up, Mom's family often moved around due to my grandfather being in the RCAF. Mom and her family spent many years on air force bases, first in Clinton, Ontario, and then in Portage la Prairie, Manitoba. As youngsters in a family of six children, they were always together. They took local family vacations and day trips whenever Bob was off work. Outings often involved one cooler in the trunk and all eight family members piling into Bob's blue Volkswagen Beetle. The younger children would sit on laps, no seat belts, with not a care in the world.

When Mom was a teenager, the family lived in a small bungalow. With Nanna, Bob, Mom's grandpa (also named Robert), six kids and one bathroom, a schedule was necessary. Every Saturday was bath time for the younger siblings. Mom, Lynda, and Robin bathed Sunday nights and then Nanna would do their hair with rollers while sitting in front of the TV watching *The Ed Sullivan Show*.

As Mom grew up, her hair became one of her standout features. Mom was glamorous and daring with her haircuts, always willing to take risks trying out new colours. She was light blonde as a young child and, rumour has it, she was a dark blonde naturally as an adult, but had dyed her hair for so long that no one is really sure. One of her favourite hairstyles was a timeless, short hairdo inspired by Petula Clark—one of Mom's favourite singers. She took her little sister Laurel to see her in concert, and Mom knew every word to every song and sang at the top of her lungs.

In 1965, the family moved to Toronto. At this point, Mom decided not to go back to school. She was a few credits shy of graduating, but Ontario had grade 13 and Mom was not interested. Instead, she decided to join the workforce. Mom found a job first as a transport dispatcher with King Transport and later a clerical role with Bell Canada with her sister Lynda. Mom and Lynda lived together, commuting every day to and from work.

Mom dated off and on in her teens and by her early 20s was even engaged twice, but neither stuck. One engagement just fizzled out, and the other ended because the man's family didn't approve as Mom wasn't Japanese. Then, in the summer of 1970, our mom and dad were introduced by mutual friends and started dating. They were like two pieces of a puzzle, they just fit. It wasn't long before Dad was part of the family. Mom appreciated that he understood her family and Mom's close relationship with Nanna.

On September 19, 1970, Mom was at home with her younger siblings while Nanna was out for her regular Saturday errands, grocery shopping and getting her hair done. There was a knock at the door, and when Mom answered she found two police officers standing there. They had come to deliver the unfathomable news that Mom's brother Bobby, then 19, had been killed in a car accident.

Mom was the one who had to tell Nanna that her son had died. This devastating news took a toll on the family, a tragedy that shook them to their core. They were missing one of their own, and Mom and her siblings had lost their brother. It was during this time that Nanna came to rely on Mom even more. This became the catalyst to what would be fundamental for the family for generations—that there is nothing more important or stronger than family.

After dating for about six months, Mom and Dad's relationship grew more serious, and they began to talk about getting married. They thought a wedding would be a distraction from their grief, and since the whole family would already be together over Christmas, they decided to get married on Boxing Day, 1970. Anyone who has woken up on Boxing Day, exhausted from the Christmas festivities the day before, will wonder how they managed a wedding. It was a small affair, and the day proved to be very emotional for all.

Mom and Dad's relationship was strong; Dad was there through Mom losing her brother and stayed by her side. This was where my mom found her path; it was with my dad. They had a deep respect for each other. They were equals. My grandfather once told me that our mom and dad had a once-in-a-lifetime kind of love.

But no one is naïve enough to think anything is perfect, as even the strongest relationships have their moments. One evening, Dad asked Mom to make his mother's 'mince and tatties' recipe (ground beef and potatoes). She obliged and asked dad what he thought after his first few bites, to which he replied that it wasn't as good as his mother's. That would prove to be the last bite he would take as the meal was taken and tossed away. Did I mention that Mom was a redhead at one point? It may have been an 'out of a box' red, but there was a temper there that fit the typical redhead. Dad would never repeat that error of judgement.

After a couple of years enjoying being newlyweds, one thing Mom wanted desperately was to be a mother. In 1973, I was born. Then, in 1975, my brother Benjamin was born. Mom chose to stay home with us while we were little. Mom was playful and affectionate, but also strict. Over the next few years, we would move several times—Scarborough, Sudbury, Oshawa, and eventually we landed in Pickering. Even in the chaos with young kids, no matter where we lived, our house was always clean. Mom was a neat freak and liked order. There was always a long list of chores on Sunday morning, and once a bed was made, you were best to sit on the floor, for fear of displacing the bedspread.

Mom was supportive of where my dad needed to be for work, even though it often moved them away from her family. Fortunately, in Pickering, Mom was near family again. We lived next door to her sister Robin and daughters for eight years. During that time, as the family expanded, the family continued to get together. There was always a lot of noise, laughter, singing, and dancing. Petula Clark would be cranked up loud with Mom belting out the words and dancing around the house.

This was a very happy time. Mom had many friends, went back to work part-time in retail, and was close to family. Mom and Robin were able to spend more time together and developed a strong friendship. They spent many afternoons out front of our houses, enjoying a shandy or two, talking and laughing for hours. This time, living next door to each other fostered a deep closeness between families that extended well into the future.

In 1985, Mom discovered a lump in her breast, and the test results showed that it was breast cancer. She had a mastectomy and began treatment. This was before much was known about the disease and the development of personalized treatment options. In 1986, the family moved from Pickering to Ottawa for Dad's work. It was difficult for Mom to move away from her family, but we travelled back and forth frequently, and Nanna and Mom would speak every Sunday evening for hours. Mom was more than a daughter to Nanna; she was her rock and vice versa.

Four years later, in 1989, the cancer returned. It had metastasized to the brain, lungs, and bones, and her time was limited. Devastation rang through the family. For her two children, this was incomprehensible. Realizing that she was dying, Mom had photos of herself framed and wrote a message on the back for each of us. It is hard to imagine how difficult this would have been for her, knowing she wouldn't see her children grow up. Our mother passed away early in the morning of August 15, 1989, when I was 16 and my brother 14.

Nanna would say that what got her through losing Mom was focusing on all the years she may not have had her, given that Mom almost died at six months old. Instead of thinking of the future she lost with Mom, she was grateful for the forty-three years she did have—forty-three years of making memories as a family. Every day since losing Mom, I have treasured the message she left on the back of my photo. *Always remember I love you.*

PENNY, 1966, WILLOWDALE, ONTARIO

Author Reflection - Amanda McNally
White Rock, BC, Canada

When I was first approached with the opportunity to write my mother's story, I knew it was something I had to do, but I didn't realize how extremely difficult it would be. Those who have experienced early mother loss have their own unique challenges when writing their mother's story. For me, I don't have many clear memories before the age of twelve. I'm sure a therapist would have a field day with that. I have feelings and flashes of memories tied to pictures or songs. It was intimidating to the point of almost paralyzing trying to figure out where to start or even how to start.

My brother and I were teenagers when our mom passed away. There is so much I wish I could go back and do differently. Regrets are heavy to carry all your life. I wish I'd talked more with my mom, asked more questions, had been more curious as to who she was, what her life had been like before me. I wish I had the chance to know her as a woman and experience the closeness that my mom and Nanna had. Taking on the challenge of writing her story helped me to feel closer to her. I learned many things that I didn't know before and realized how many traits we have in common.

I recently heard a saying that resonated with me: "from pain to purpose." I have spent my career using what happened to my mom to help others, first working at a cancer non-profit, educating men and women on the importance of cancer risk reduction and early detection. Most recently, I joined an organization that supports our community through grief and palliative services. My career has been therapeutic for me, trying to make some good from the tragedy in my life. I have spoken about her illness, her death, and my grief to help others. The opportunity to write her story allowed me to focus on her life, who she was, and it has been a heartbreakingly beautiful process.

The importance of family and the closeness that my grandparents fostered all those years ago is clearly apparent today, right down to the youngest generation. Those are the lessons we've been taught from our family's losses.

I find myself often commenting that this time in my life now feels like the hardest time without her. I am now a mother and an aunt. I wish desperately that my children, my nieces, and nephew could know their Nanna. I wish we could see them all playing together. They would bring her so much joy. The Story of Penny is for them so that they can know their Nanna. This story is also a reminder that life is short, but when we remember those we've loved and lost and tell their stories, they live on in us forever.

20 | Michelle Hohn's Story of Florence

I sat on the edge of the turquoise bathtub, my tiny bum seated on the chenille mat and sock feet dangling above the linoleum tile. My mother's focus alternated between her task at hand and her smiling eyes finding mine in the mirror as I watched.

"You press down gently, but firmly—like this—for about thirty seconds," she said as she held her eyelash curler in place.

This was one of our girl rituals. It was never too early, she would say, to learn how to take care of your skin or apply cosmetics. There was something truly hypnotizing about watching her transform into a glamourous, powdery-smelling enchantress before going out for the evening. Mom bought me my own gloss so we could do our lips together, standing side-by-side in front of the mirror—hers a frosty, bright pink and mine with a tint of colour and delicious candy smell.

I was happy for my parents whenever they went out; my five-year-old emotions aligned with Mom's excitement about the night ahead. I would transport to her destination in my mind's eye after their goodbye kisses, believing her dreams were coming true through good times she told me that I too would enjoy when I reached womanhood. She was beautiful, and quite simply, my everything.

Back then, there was no reason to believe that anything could ever go wrong.

Florence Lillian was the eldest of two daughters born to Polish immigrants, Vladislava ("Lillian") Palkowski and Alfons Mackiewicz. After settling on their respective family homesteads in Canada in the mid-30s, Lillian and Alfons met through mutual friends in Coal Valley, Alberta. They later moved to and were married in Edmonton in 1939; he a furrier, and she a homemaker. Their house was warm and welcoming, filled with family and friends, accordion music, and the savoury smells of old-country cooking—cabbage rolls, beet soup, and the bacon and onion steam of an endless supply of perogies.

Florence was born on February 2, 1941 and was raised with a modest kind of abundance—love and laughter. She was a happy, chubby, healthy baby, albeit choosey with her affections. As a toddler, little Florence preferred the outdoors, entertaining herself in the garden amongst the rows of flowers (roses being her favourite) or setting up tea service for imaginary friends in the shady grass beneath the apple tree.

Florence's sister, Zenna, was born in 1944, when Florence was three. She took being charged with her little sister's care seriously, bringing Zenna with her everywhere, never making her feel like a tag-along, protectively standing up for her at school, and covering for her mischief at home.

Florence's early report cards documented a creative, straight-A student, although "chatty and at times moody". She had an ear for music and took advantage of her long, slender fingers to play piano. In 1955, she received Advanced Rudiments (theory and technique) credits from the Royal Conservatory of Music. She hoped one day to teach, envisioning students coming to her home for lessons; entrepreneurial plans that would never materialize.

Maintaining the illusion of 'good girl' throughout adolescence, Florence snuck her share of lemon gin and beer, and only close friends and her sister knew that she smoked cigarettes. In a time when most girls didn't, she whispered "shit" under her breath and dated more than her parents knew about—preferring boys with convertibles.

Florence became a striking young woman—5'8", slender, and small-waisted, with pale blue eyes, a flawless complexion, and light brown hair that she kept short. Her fingernails were always painted in frosty pinks or mauves. She loved to dress in bright, fun shades—especially turquoise and pink—and she *always* dressed to go out. Her sense of style came easy; outfits, jewellery, shoes, and handbags all mixed-and-matched in a breezy way, finished with a mist of Tabu. Florence's legs were long and her walk graceful, and she had an enviable skin tone that transformed each summer into a Mediterranean bronze.

Roses remained her favourite flower and, just like baby Florence, she continued to be selective with her affections into adulthood—quiet and reserved until she got to know someone. To those few, Florence was described as a warm and loyal friend and confidante. Many spoke of Florence's presence, a lightness and elegance that turned heads when she walked into a room, alongside the tell-tale jangle of her charm bracelet. She had a spirited laugh, a good sense of humour, and her social trademark was sharp wit and offering a snappy comeback. She loved to dance, belonged to the curling club and bowling league, and became a good billiards and card player, especially hearts.

After graduating grade 12 with honours in 1958, Florence surprised everyone by declaring she did not plan to go to university. She felt she already had a good job as a keypunch operator at Medical Services Inc (MSI) and did not wish to waste her time or her parents' money. MSI was where Florence had met Edna, who became her closest friend. Living just two blocks apart, Edna and Florence walked to and from work together every day. Back then, women didn't wear sneakers or loafers, so they traversed the miles in stiletto heels and pencil skirts in all weather conditions, including snow and ice, over difficult and sometimes precarious terrain like gravel roads and railroad tracks.

Florence met the man who would become her husband through work in 1964, when they were both 23. Promoted to department supervisor, Florence's job included coordinating with International Business Machines technicians for maintenance and repairs. Gerald Wayne Hohn was 6'4", handsome, with black hair, blue-grey eyes, and large, capable hands. By day he was professional and clean cut; off-hours, he wore a leather jacket, played guitar, and drove a black convertible MG. On his second maintenance call, Gerry asked Florence out to a company hayride. Around this same time, Florence stopped seeing a man named George, turning him down gently when he came by the house with a ring.

Florence and Gerry dated for over a year, enjoying movies, parties, picnics, and particularly Stage West Dinner Theatre before getting engaged. They also travelled; destinations like Jasper National Park or Radium Hot Springs were modest, but some were quite exciting for the time, including Montreal and the 1964 New York World's Fair.

With Florence's savings as their down payment, she and Gerry purchased and moved into their first home together (against both common practice and the views of her Catholic parents) with their cat, "Puss." They married soon after, on November 6, 1965. While Florence had always dreamed of visiting Hawaii, the newlyweds honeymooned in Yellowstone National Park the following spring. She meticulously documented their first three years of marriage in photo albums filled with travel adventures, house parties, and holiday dinners with family and friends, all captioned with exquisite handwriting in the white borders.

The couple's firstborn, Michelle Marie, arrived just after Christmas in 1968. Mom left her job to take care of our home and family, a role she took immense pride in—always thinking of her family first. I had my parents' attention to myself for close to five years before my brother, Jeffery David, was born in early 1974. Mom loved her little king with all her heart. Her family, she told her mother, was now complete.

Mom was a strict disciplinarian, but sometimes she surprised me by respecting my budding decisions; like when I told her I was not interested in ballet lessons or becoming a Brownie. Some of her rules included, "Make your bed before breakfast," "No dawdling," and "Be quiet during *The Dating Game*." She would scold us for sneaking cinnamon Dentyne or mint Tic-Tacs from her purse and she did fuss about things being 'just so.' Our childhood home, for example, had two Christmas trees—one upstairs, carefully adorned with glass ornaments and individually-placed strands of tinsel, versus the basement kid's tree for our dried macaroni decorations and construction paper garland.

Mom proudly took my brother and me to parks and swimming

pools in summers and to skating rinks or tobogganing in winters. She wanted us to get fresh air, use our imaginations, and play. Knowing there would be plenty of time later in life for domestic chores, she often shooed us from the sewing room or kitchen but would always call us back to lick the sweet remnants off the cake beaters or to keep her company while she did her hair or makeup.

Mom was extremely close with her parents, and they adored her. Countless hours were spent at their chrome and Formica kitchen table where Granny would iron and talk in Polish while Mom and Zenna sipped Nescafe and scanned the latest Loblaws flyer. Grandpa's hearing was bad, so Mom included him in other ways, like kissing the top of his head while he sat nearby in his TV recliner. In 1978, she showed her devotion through a Father's Day radio contest. The challenge was to describe your dad in one word. Mom won the grand prize—an electric lawn mower—by calling in the word "irreplaceable." Grandpa cried.

Budgeting was an ongoing priority: Mom trimmed my hair (a regular source of conflict when my bangs came out crooked), sewed window coverings and clothing, custom-tailored Dad's suits, baked our birthday 'money cakes', and was a disciplined coupon clipper. Mom's one permissible luxury was her mink coat, which she proudly donned during the deep freeze of Alberta winters.

My parents enjoyed the popular music of the day, but Mom seemed to *need* music. As soon as Dad left for work, she would turn on the radio, filling the house with songs with a beat like the "Lido Shuffle", and some days we'd drop everything and dance. She'd call out to turn down the volume while she talked on the telephone, perched on a barstool with her index finger twisting through the long, coiled cord. Music was always on in the car too, where Mom would sing and tap her rings against the steering wheel while she drove.

Summers were spent at the family cabin at Wizard Lake; fun and relaxing times enjoying water sports by day and bonfires at night with roasted hot dogs and marshmallows. Dad was an accomplished water skier, and Mom liked to float on the Dad-made barge, accompanied by a Caesar and a Harlequin romance.

Our life may have been simple, but it was predictable. And stable. Until 1977, when Mom discovered a lump in her left breast. In what may have been the most defining moment of her life, she hesitated. We will never know for certain why. We could perhaps imagine the intense trepidation she may have felt. Or we could look to Mom's only model for what might happen in a similar situation, as her uncle had left her Aunt Val and their children, stating that he "married a whole woman, not half of one," on his way out the door when Val needed a mastectomy. Mom finally confided in Granny, but it was a full year before she sought medical attention. Our competent, intelligent, detail-oriented, take-care-of-everyone-else Mom somehow neglected to take care of herself.

After receiving a biopsy and breast cancer diagnosis on her birthday in 1978, Mom quickly underwent surgery, radiation, and chemotherapy. Although outwardly positive, Mom's medical records would later reveal that this was unrealistic; her situation had been aggressively metastatic from the start. Mom died on March 26, 1980, at the age of 39, when I was eleven and my brother Jeff only six.

I imagine Mom's version of the afterlife as the Hawaiian paradise she longed to visit. Perhaps she is strolling on a white sand beach, the skirt of her sundress billowing in the tropical breeze. Maybe she is raising a lemon gin to a glorious sunset from a veranda framed by palm fronds, enveloped in the fragrance of tuber rose, to mark what could have been her 81st birthday this year.

FLORENCE, APRIL 1964, EDMONTON, ALBERTA

Author Reflection - Michelle Hohn
Nanoose Bay, BC, Canada

The *Gone Too Soon* anthology represents my third round of *My Mother's Story* reflection. I originally wrote "The Story of Florence" in 2015 and uploaded it to the online archive. It was a powerful— and quite unexpected—way to 'un-disappear' my mom from the loss, grief, and bereavement carpet she had been swept under in the 80s. After her passing, the very mention of the woman who bore and raised us to that point transitioned from hushed tones and discouraged looks to entirely taboo. Photos of her were taken down, and we were expected to carry on as though nothing had happened. Thirty-five years later, *My Mother's Story* was one of the first venues that gave me permission to speak freely and share abundantly about my mother's life—it was the actual task at hand!

Before I began drafting, I had a reasonable amount of memories, and a small, yet precious collection of sentimental items, like some of her costume jewellery, a set of Polish crystal wine glasses and, of course, her photo albums. But these were just fragments of her life—remnants to cling to in moments of yearning; her belongings the touchstone of proof that she once existed.

It was through my research and writing process that details about Mom's existence, as opposed to her absence, began to weave together in one place. She started to manifest more strongly and more tangibly in my heart, and her re-emergence was a delightful mouse-click away for anyone who wished to learn about her experiences, her loves, her values, and the decisions that made her who she was for the short time that she did have with us. I not only felt I had honoured her, but also re-established a sense of Motherline wisdom and belonging that I had been denied for decades.

Really knowing my mom also meant getting to know so much more about myself, and, to use her contest-winning word, my "irreplaceable" connection to her. I could suddenly feel her alongside me during witty banter amongst friends, when doting on my guy, or when getting ready to go out. I could laugh and accept that fussing with the Christmas decorations until they are 'just so' is because being *that* particular, is embedded in my DNA.

In 2017, I revisited "The Story of Florence" and felt compelled to make one major revision. I replaced the introduction with a sweet mother-daughter moment that took hypno-regression therapy to shake loose. My mom's story had not changed, but I had. As an adult narrator bereaved in childhood, my loss and grief processing and meaning-making landscape were shifting, and thus, so did my selection of what I felt should be included in her story. With healing hindsight, I could see how my previous opening revealed more about my pain surrounding her death than it did about her life. I became more drawn to a scene that transported me to the living essence of my mother and the felt experiences I know I had as a child.

For this anthology, I entered yet another phase of reflection. I had no new facts, memories, or family lore to infuse, but with the sharpest edges of the pain of childhood loss dissipating, I actually began to have fun. I scanned her story for passages I could trade-out to make room for more of Mom's trademark 'spice'. And I dove back into her photo albums knowing I could find a picture that captured the moxie of her youth. I still adore the image that Dad snapped of me and Mom in our fur coats in the winter of '73, which accompanied the 2015 version of the story, but I now feel increasingly comfortable letting Mom take center stage; shining the light more fully on her while I step out of the frame.

Akin to the other authors in this collection—and indeed others who have experienced early parental loss—my mother's death had life-altering, life-long impacts on *me*, but writing her story was a way to shift away from my feelings, to reveal and celebrate *her* life. This slowly led me from a place of feeling she was nowhere, to one where I can feel Mom everywhere and see her in everything—a new lens that I am grateful to look through.

The workshops and sessions where we shared our expressive writing with other authors have been an essential part of the process. Bringing our mothers back to life out loud and bearing witness to each woman's story is incredibly healing. This may seem matter of fact or obvious, but for those experiencing early mother loss, hearing her name and our truths out loud for the first time can be intensely illuminating—the electric shock of resonance in finding others who just *get* this.

Now, if someone asks what I learned from my mother or in what ways I am like her, I can answer with confidence and pride. I know how we are different and how we are alike. I no longer feel somehow untethered or the quiet, yet constant hum of lack and longing in the background. That space between where I am and where I feel Mom is, is now incredibly close, instead of incurably vast. I have always had a mom and continue to have a mom. She is just no longer with us on this physical plane.

Dr. Evelyn Bassoff, psychologist and author of *Mothering Ourselves: Help and Healing for Adult Daughters* tells us that "…the child [of early loss] misses the vital experience of being affirmed, admired, seen, appreciated, heard, understood, and known as s/he is" (page 6). While this may be heartbreaking and irreversibly true, it gives me great comfort knowing that my mother's story has enabled me to bestow the gift of this vital experience *to* my mom.

Through this work, my mother, Florence, can be understood and known as she was while she lived; she can be seen and admired in the hearts of those who loved her; her presence is affirmed, bound in an inspiring and healing collection containing immense transformation, courage, gratitude, and resiliency; nestled amongst the lives of other extraordinary women gone too soon.

SPECIAL THANKS

It takes many people to believe in a project like this and give it (and us) life and support—sometimes with encouragement, sometimes with time, and sometimes with cash.

Our heartfelt thanks to:

~ All of our courageous, authentic, and compassionate authors. It was through your brave efforts and conscientious work that we were able to create a genuine community of healing and support while creating this important book. And to your mothers—who bestowed upon you the qualities, abilities, and ultimate strength you needed to be able to share their lives and your healing journey with others.

~ Our sponsors, for recognizing projects like this cannot run on passion alone. Akashic Counselling, Gerald Whittall, JG Freedman, Andrea Fecko, Ken McAuliffe, and our Patreon patrons.

~ Mandy Gosling, for her sage wisdom, specialized perspective, 'heart talk', and reams of behind-the-scenes support to get us and *Gone Too Soon* to the finish line.

~ Amanda McNally, for her time and expertise spearheading our social media and digital marketing campaign.

~ Tammi Hall and Hallographix Design, for our gorgeous book cover and going above and beyond in the creation of a suite of other beautiful graphics for our use.

~ Carlyn Craig and Post Hypnotic Press, for being an amazing support and publishing mentor - from the very beginning to today.

~ Diana Reyers and Daring to Share Global, for your kind and generous guidance.

~ Alessandra Olmedo for your ongoing engagement with all-things-*My Mother's Story*, your friendship, and always being 'on deck'.

~ Current and past board members of Mothership Stories Society.

"No words can fully express my appreciation to Greg, who still patiently listens to umpteen rewrites of the same thing and reminds me every time that this work matters."

-Marilyn Norry

"My deepest love and gratitude to Fred: for being my home base and safe place through my ongoing and ever-changing journey of discovery and healing; for your unconditional support, never questioning the latest version of the path (particularly during the woo-woo segments of the exploration); and for letting me be the authentic me I need to be—or become."

-Michelle Hohn

REFERENCES

Adams, K. (1990). *Journal to the Self: Twenty-Two Paths to Personal Growth* Grand Central Publishing. New York, NY.

Adults Bereaved as Children and Grief: www.abcgrief.co.uk

Basoff, E.S. (1991). *Mothering Ourselves: Help and Healing for Adult Daughters.* New York, NY. Penguin Group.

Children and Youth Grief Network:
https://www.childrenandyouthgriefnetwork.com

Gosling, M. (2016). Understanding Childhood Parental Bereavement from a Psychological and Spiritual Perspective. Unpublished manuscript. MA Transpersonal Counselling and Psychotherapy (CCPE), University of Northampton.

Judi's House / JAG Institute for Grieving Children and Families:
https://judishouse.org

Klass, D., Sliverman, P., & Nickman, S. (Eds). (1996). Continuing Bonds: New Understandings of Grief. Washington, DC. Taylor & Francis.

Lowinsky, N.R. (1992). *The Motherline: Every Woman's Journey to Find Her Female Roots.* Published simultaneously in Canada, the United Kingdom and the United States of America. Fisher King Press.

Norry, M. (Ed). (2012). *My Mother's Story: The Originals.* New Westminster, BC. Mothership Stories Society.

Pennebaker, J.W. (2004). *Writing to Heal: A Guided Journal for Recovering from Trauma & Emotional Upheaval.* USA. New Harbinger Publications.

Pennebaker, J.W. & Smyth, J.M. (2016). *Opening Up by Writing It Down: How Expressive Writing Improves Health and Heals Emotional Pain* (3rd ed). USA. New Harbinger Publications.

The Childhood Bereavement Network:
https://childhoodbereavementnetwork.org.uk

Worden, J. W. (2018) *Grief Counseling and Grief Therapy: A Handbook for the Mental Health Practitioner,* Fifth Edition, New York, NY. Springer Publishing Company.

Yalom, I. (2005). *The Theory and Practice of Group Psychotherapy,* Fifth Edition. New York, NY. Basic Books.